Learning Disabilities

Developmental Clinical Psychology and Psychiatry Series

Series Editor: Alan E. Kazdin, Yale University

Recent volumes in this series . . .

Learning Disabilities
A Neuropsychological Perspective

Byron P. Rourke
Jerel E. Del Dotto

Volume 30.
Developmental Clinical Psychology and Psychiatry

 SAGE Publications
International Educational and Professional Publisher
Thousand Oaks   London   New Delhi

For information address:

SAGE Publications, Inc.
2455 Teller Road
Thousand Oaks, California 91320

SAGE Publications Ltd.
6 Bonhill Street
London EC2A 4PU
United Kingdom

SAGE Publications India Pvt. Ltd.
M-32 Market
Greater Kailash I
New Delhi 110048 India

Printed in the United States of America

Library of Congress Cataloging-in-Publication Data

Rourke, Byron P. (Byron Patrick), 1939-
    Learning disabilities: a neuropsychological perspective / Byron
P. Rourke, Jerel E. Del Dotto.
        p. cm.—(Developmental clinical psychology and psychiatry:
v. 30)
    Includes bibliographical references and index.
    ISBN 0-8039-5353-4 (cl.)—ISBN 0-8039-5354-2 (pbk.)
    1. Learning disabilities—Physiological aspects. 2. Learning
disabilities—Classification. 3. Learning disabilities—
Psychological aspects. 4. Learning disabled children. I. Del
Dotto, Jerel E. II. Title. III. Series.
    [DNLM: 1. Learning Disorders. 2. Brain Diseases—in infancy &
childhood. W1 DE997NC v. 30 1994]
RJ496.L4R68 1994
616.85'889—dc20
DNLM/DLC   94-65

94 95 96 97 10 9 8 7 6 5 4 3 2 1

Sage Production Editor: Diane S. Foster

CONTENTS

for Bryan, Dom, Joshua, Kathryn, and Sara

SERIES EDITOR'S
INTRODUCTION

Interest in child development and adjustment is by no means new. Yet, only recently has the study of children benefited from advances in both clinical and scientific research. Advances in the social and biological sciences, the emergence of disciplines and subdisciplines that focus extensively on childhood and adolescence, and greater appreciation of the impact of such influences as the family, peers, and school have helped accelerate research on developmental psychopathology. Apart from interest in the study of child development and adjustment for its own sake, the need to address clinical problems of adulthood naturally draws one to investigate precursors in childhood and adolescence.

Within a relatively brief period, the study of psychopathology among children and adolescents has proliferated considerably. Several different professional journals, annual book series, and handbooks devoted entirely to the study of children and adolescents and their adjustment document the proliferation of work in the field. Nevertheless, there is a paucity of resource material that presents information in an authoritative, systematic, and disseminable fashion. There is a need within the field to convey the latest developments and to represent different disciplines, approaches, and conceptual views to the topics of childhood and adolescent adjustment and maladjustment.

The Sage Series on **Developmental Clinical Psychology and Psychiatry** is designed to serve uniquely several needs of the field. The Series encompasses individual monographs prepared by experts in the fields of clinical child psychology, child psychiatry, child development, and related disciplines. The primary focus is on developmental psychopathology, which refers broadly here to the diagnosis, assessment, treatment, and prevention of problems that arise in the period from infancy through adolescence. A working assumption of the Series is that understanding, identifying, and treating problems of youth must draw on multiple disciplines and diverse views within a given discipline.

The task for individual contributors is to present the latest theory and research on various topics, including specific types of dysfunction, diagnostic and treatment approaches, and special problem areas that affect adjustment. Core topics within clinical work are addressed by the Series. Authors are asked to bridge potential theory, research, and clinical practice and to outline the current status and future directions. The goals of the Series and the tasks presented to individual contributors are demanding. We have been extremely fortunate in recruiting leaders in the fields who have been able to translate their recognized scholarship and expertise into highly readable works on contemporary topics.

Byron P. Rourke and Jerel E. Del Dotto examine learning disabilities among children and adolescents. The book provides a neuropsychological perspective as a way of integrating research and guiding clinical intervention. Many topics are covered, including characteristics and descriptive features of learning disability, subtypes, domains of social functioning, assessment of assets and deficits, and methods of intervention, to sample only a small portion of the areas included in the book. An excellent interplay of research and clinical work pervades the book. The accumulated and programmatic findings from research on the nature and characteristics of learning disabilities as well as advances in assessment are applied clinically in detailed case studies. Also, how to intervene with one subtype of learning disabled youth is covered in an appendix to provide concrete guidelines for clinical work. The book is superb in its scope, statement of the issues, and guidelines for both improving our understanding of dysfunction and for intervening.

—*Alan E. Kazdin, Ph.D.*

FOREWORD

Some of the material in this book has been adapted from several of our previous works, including the following: Rourke and Del Dotto (1992) and Rourke and Fuerst (1991, 1992). We are most grateful to our colleagues who participated in these and the other collaborative works cited throughout this book.

1

HISTORICAL BACKGROUND AND BASIC ISSUES

This work is designed for child clinical psychologists and others whose professional practice brings them into contact with children and adolescents who exhibit learning disabilities (LD). Our aim is to present some of the relevant research in the area of LD and to draw out the implications of this research for clinical practice. The book is organized in terms of a frankly neuropsychological approach to the topic because, in our view, this constitutes the most comprehensive perspective from which to structure this field.

The first chapter deals with some basic issues in the study of LD and a summary and critique of some of the many viewpoints regarding research and professional practice within the field of LD. Subtypes of LD and dimensions of psychosocial functioning are dealt with in Chapters 2 and 3, respectively. This is followed by an introduction to what we consider to be a comprehensive and cohesive model of neuropsychological assessment and intervention for children with LD. The final section of the work contains detailed case studies that exemplify the principal subtypes of LD that have been identified, and the manner in which an analysis of neuropsychological assets and deficits can lead to a comprehensive understanding of the child as well as methods of intervention that would be consistent with such an understanding. These cases are designed to illustrate the application of general principles derived from research to the clinical imperatives of day-to-day practice with youngsters who exhibit LD.

GENERAL HISTORICAL BACKGROUND

Definitions

As a working hypothesis, many researchers and clinicians propose that there is a biological basis (i.e., some form of mild or subtle brain dysfunction) for the set of developmental disorders known as LD. This hypothesis is clearly reflected in the exclusionary definition that is typically applied to the term. In this context, an individual is considered to be learning disabled when he or she encounters significant difficulty in acquiring one or more basic academic skills in an age-appropriate manner—usually determined by a standardized measure of academic achievement—a failure that cannot be accounted for on the basis of mental retardation; sensory impairment; frank neurological disease or disorder; emotional disturbance; or inadequate exposure to appropriate linguistic, cultural, or educational experiences.

There are, however, very evident problems in *assuming* this biological basis, as opposed to *demonstrating* it (Rourke, 1975). Furthermore, there is a sound basis for *including* brain damage, disorder, and dysfunction (e.g., significant craniocerebral trauma) in the etiology of some forms of LD (Rourke, 1989). Discussions of these and related definitional issues are dealt with throughout this work, and an explicit set of definitions that we propose is contained in Chapter 5. (The interested reader may wish to peruse Chapter 5 at this point to gain familiarity with these definitions that we view as the culmination— rather than the beginning—of inquiry within this area.)

Prevalence

Because there exists no clear-cut, consensually validated discriminative designation of LD (i.e., there is no known biological or agreed-upon behavioral marker that clearly dichotomizes the learning disabled from the non-learning disabled), efforts to determine the prevalence of the disorder have proven to be problematic. According to the Commission on Emotional and Learning Disorders in Children (CELDIC Report, 1970), it was estimated that the number of "exceptional" children in Canada requiring specialized remedial assistance ranged from 10% to 15%. This commission, in presenting their report, cited similar estimates for Great Britain (14%), France (12% to 14%), and the United States (10% to 15%). However, the reader will immediately recognize that such estimates include some undefined proportion of children who display academic underachievement because of emotional disturbance, cultural and/or linguistic deprivation, mental retardation, and other specific developmental disorders—in other words, children who do not meet the usual exclusionary criteria defining LD, as cited above.

Genetics

The frequent observation that LD often run in families and that certain learning problems (e.g., especially those of a language or language-related nature) are more common in male children (Ansara, Geschwind, Galaburda, Albert, & Gartrell, 1981; Rourke, 1978b; Singer, Westphal, & Niswander, 1968) has no doubt stimulated, at least in part, the search for evidence to support a genetic mechanism of transmission. In his classic study of so-called congenital word blindness, Hallgren (1950) concluded that there was a high probability that this specific form of dyslexia was determined by a dominant mode of inheritance. In a related study, Hermann (1959) reported 100% concordance in monozygotic twins and 33% concordance among dyzygotic twins for congenital word blindness.

Owen (1978), however, in her review of research on genetic aspects, stated that the most one could conclude is that certain types of dyslexia may be transmitted via multifactorial inheritance, that is, expression and severity is a complex interaction between genetic predisposition (probable multiple genes) and environmental experience. Thus, until we are able to define precisely the various phenotypic expressions of LD, attempts to study the genetic characteristics are, at best, premature and, at worst, counterproductive.

This challenge has been addressed admirably in some excellent recent work (e.g., DeFries, Fulker, & LaBuda, 1987; Smith, Goldgar, Pennington, Kimberlin, & Lubs, 1986) that has utilized fairly precise phenotypical classifications of disabled reading in an attempt to determine their genetic implications. The upshot of this genre of sophisticated investigation will, undoubtedly, have a profound impact on our understanding of reading disabilities and other forms of LD.

Other Biological Dimensions

It has been shown by a number of investigators that prenatal, perinatal, and neonatal complications are more prominent in the clinical histories of "dyslexic" children as compared to normal readers (Galante, Flye, & Stevens, 1972; Kawi & Pasamanick, 1959). There is also an extensive electrophysiological literature in which a number of investigators have reported differences in evoked potentials among various subtypes of children with LD (e.g., Bakker, Licht, Kok, & Bouma, 1980; Dool, Stelmack, & Rourke, 1993; Grunau & Low, 1987; Lovrich & Stamm, 1983; Miles & Stelmack, in press). However, no study in this rather extensive literature clearly elucidates the nature of underlying mechanism(s) of learning disability. Indeed, as Fletcher and Taylor (1984) have so eloquently argued, there exists no specific set of brain-behavior relationships by which cerebral dysfunction and developmental disorders can be validated. Nevertheless, it is clear that continued advances in research on evoked potentials would be expected to have a significant impact upon assessment of children with LD (Dool et al., 1993).

With these general observations regarding definition, incidence, and biology/psychophysiology as background, we turn now to a discussion of the pros and cons of the predominant research and theoretical positions that have held sway in the field of LD over the past 35 years.

LEARNING DISABILITIES AS AN UNIVOCAL, HOMOGENEOUS DISORDER

Early work in the neuropsychology of LD focused almost exclusively on the study of reading disability (Benton, 1975; Rourke, 1978a). With a few notable exceptions, this research—and, for that matter, practice—was characterized by the "contrasting-groups" or "comparative populations" (Applebee, 1971) investigative strategy that was the almost exclusive approach adopted by North American and European researchers. Studies involving comparisons of groups of youngsters with supposed LD and groups of age- and otherwise-matched "normal" controls were employed to determine *the* deficit(s) that characterize the neuropsychological ability structure of *the* learning-disabled child (Doehring, 1978). The use of this method for the determination of the neuropsychological assets and deficits of children with LD assumed, implicitly or explicitly, that such children formed a univocal, homogeneous diagnostic entity.

This approach was also characterized by rather narrow samplings of areas of human performance that were thought to be related to the learning (primarily reading) disability. For example, some researchers who were convinced that a deficiency in memory (or perception, or any other important cognitive function) formed the basis for LD in youngsters would follow a rather straightforward research tack: That is, they would measure and compare "memory" in groups of children with LD and matched control children. Almost without fail, the conclusion of such a research effort was that children with LD were deficient in memory; this led to the inference that it was this deficient memory that was the cause of the children's LD. In fact, the only crucial variable that, typically, influenced the results of such studies was the severity of the learning deficit of the subjects with LD studied: The more severe the learning deficit, the more likely it was that the contrasting groups would differ in memory, perception, or any number of other variables.

Such research was periodically seen as somewhat shortsighted and inconclusive when it could be demonstrated, for example, that disabled learners were more deficient in "auditory memory" than they were in "visual memory." This constituted something of an advance in the field, because a rather more comprehensive sampling of skills and abilities was undertaken in this sort of study. There remained the commitment to the contrasting-groups methodology, however, and there was one other complicating factor that crept into the considerations of investigators in the field. This factor could best be described as the developmental dimension. Specifically, it became clear to some that one "obtained" significant differences between contrasting groups of disabled and normal readers on some variables and not on others as an apparent function of the age at which the children were studied. Thus an example of the next advance that took place in this research tradition was to compare groups of younger and older children on auditory and visual memory tasks to determine if the main effects (for auditory and visual memory) and the interactions (with age) were significant.

Even with these advances, however, there remained the reluctance of those who adopted this essentially narrow nomothetic approach to engage in the comprehensive analysis of the assets and deficits of individual children with LD. For example, it was rarely the case that investigators would report results of individual cases in their studies of auditory and visual memory (or any other variable), even though this is very simply accomplished (see Czudner & Rourke, 1972; Rourke & Czudner, 1972, for examples of how individual results can be reported in such studies). In the absence of this level of analysis, the field was left with group results that may not reflect how all individuals within the group performed. Some critics of this nomothetic approach to the understanding of LD in children adopted a position that was quite antithetical to it, namely, one that is best described as an "idiosyncratic" or "idiographic" approach to the field.

LEARNING DISABILITIES AS
AN IDIOSYNCRATIC DISORDER

As was the case in the history of the study of frank brain damage in youngsters, there have long been investigators in the field of LD who would maintain that persons so designated exhibit very unique, idiosyncratic, nongeneralizable origins, characteristics, and reactions to their afflictions and, as such, must be treated in an idiographic manner. Investigators of this ilk would suggest that the single-case study is the only viable means for discovering valid scientific information. They would also argue that the important dimensions of this disorder are individualized to the extent that meaningful generalizations are virtually impossible.

It is clear that this point of view contrasts sharply and in almost all respects with the contrasting-groups position outlined above. This nomothetic/idiographic debate is not unique to the study of LD and frankly brain-damaged individuals. Indeed, it is a controversy that has been with us since the dawn of empirical psychology. (A particularly poignant and insightful characterization of this nomothetic/idiographic controversy in the entire field of clinical neuropsychology has been presented by Reitan [1974].)

CRITIQUE OF THE CONTRASTING-GROUPS
AND IDIOSYNCRATIC APPROACHES

Contrasting-Groups Approach

As suggested above, studies within this tradition served to do little more than produce a lengthy catalog of variables that differentiate so-called learning-disabled from normal children (Rourke, 1978a). Considered as a whole, the results of this corpus of research made it abundantly evident that virtually any single measure of perceptual, psycholinguistic, or higher order cognitive skill could be used to illustrate the superiority of normal children over comparable groups of children diagnosed as having LD. It was simply a question of utilizing groups of children with varying severities of LD in order to generate results compatible with the investigator's pet theory.

Although the essential bankruptcy of this approach has been known for some time (Rourke, 1975), there are many who persist in the utilization of the comparative-populations or contrasting-groups meth-

odology, with all of the limitations that such a methodology involves—
not only with respect to research findings, but also with respect to
model-building and theory development. This mode of approach to
research—aimed at the identification of *the* supposed cognitive and
other correlates of children with LD—has not been terribly contributory: For example, the results of many studies are trivial, contradictory
to one another, and not supported in replication attempts; there is little
to suggest that the factors identified as "characteristic" of children with
LD in these studies are related to one another in any meaningful fashion
(Rourke, 1985). In sum, the evidence regarding perceptual, cognitive,
and other forms of functioning that emerges from the contrasting-
groups approach to research is, at best, equivocal. A coherent and
meaningful pattern of neuropsychological characteristics of children
with LD does not emerge from this literature. We would maintain that
this is the case because such a univocal pattern does not obtain (much
more on this point below).

In any event, there would appear to be at least four major reasons why
the results of these studies have not been very contributory to the testing
of important hypotheses relating to the neuropsychological integrity of
youngsters with LD. These, together with some brief comments on
alternative approaches, may be summarized as follows:

1. Lack of a Conceptual Model. In the vast majority of studies that
can be characterized in terms of the comparative-populations or contrasting-groups rubric, there is an obvious absence of a comprehensive
conceptual model that could be employed to elucidate the skills involved in perception, learning, memory, and cognition and that are
deficient in children with LD. Most models that have been developed
in this genre of research bear the marks of either post hoc theorizing
about a very limited spectrum of skills and abilities or "pet" theories
derived from what are characterized as more "general" models of
perception, learning, memory, and cognition. Research that is cast in
terms of these very limited, narrow-band models and, a fortiori, research that is essentially atheoretical in nature is virtually certain to
yield a less than comprehensive explanation of LD.

As an example of an alternative to this conceptually limited approach, a componential analysis of academic and other types of learning
should sensitize the researcher to the possibility that, whereas some
subtypes of children with LD may experience learning problems because of deficiencies in certain perceptual, cognitive, or behavioral

skills, others may manifest such problems as a more direct result of attitudinal/motivational or vastly different perceptual, cognitive, or behavioral difficulties. It should also be clear that different patterns of perceptual, cognitive, and behavioral skills and abilities may encourage different types or degrees of learning difficulties. Recently, theories that emphasize this type of comprehensive, componential approach to the design of developmental neuropsychological explanatory models in this area have emerged (e.g., Fletcher & Taylor, 1984). Our own efforts in this regard (Rourke, 1976b, 1982, 1983, 1987, 1989) are described in subsequent sections of this work.

   2. *Definition of LD.* There has been no consistent formulation of the criteria for LD in the contrasting-groups genre of study. For example, most studies of this ilk employ vaguely defined or even undefined groups, and others use the ratings of teachers and other school personnel that remain otherwise unspecified. Some even employ the guidelines of a particular political jurisdiction to define LD! It is obvious that this lack of clarity and consistency has had a negative impact on the generalizability of the (limited) findings of such studies.
   Clear definitions that are amenable to consensual validation are an urgent need in this area of investigation. In this connection, it would seem patently obvious that the very definitions themselves should be a *result* of sophisticated subtype analysis rather than the starting point of such inquiry (Morris & Fletcher, 1988; Rourke, 1983, 1985; Rourke & Gates, 1981). As suggested above, it is for this reason that the discursive sections of this book *end,* rather than begin, with definitions of LD (see Chapter 5).

   3. *Developmental Considerations.* Part and parcel of the contrasting-groups approach to the study of youngsters with LD is a gross insensitivity to age differences and developmental considerations. Several studies offer support for the notion that the nature and patterning of the skill and ability deficits of (some subtypes of) children with LD vary with age (e.g., Fisk & Rourke, 1979; Fletcher & Satz, 1980; McKinney, Short, & Feagans, 1985; Morris, Blashfield, & Satz, 1986; Ozols & Rourke, 1988; Rourke, Dietrich, & Young, 1973). Because it would seem reasonable to infer that the neuropsychological functioning of (some subtypes of) children with LD varies as a function of age (considered as one index of developmental change), the aforementioned inconsistencies in contrasting-groups research results could reflect differences in the ages of the subjects employed.

Although this possibility is sometimes acknowledged by investigators who employ this type of methodology, such a realization has, until quite recently, been the exception rather than the rule. Be that as it may, it is abundantly clear that more cross-sectional and longitudinal studies are necessary in order to clarify the nature of those developmental changes that appear to take place in some children with LD. It is also clear that attention to the issues involved in the study of developmental changes in children with LD is an almost direct function of the sophistication in subtype analysis exhibited by the neuropsychological investigators in this area (see Morris, Blashfield, & Satz, 1986, for an especially good example of perspicacious sensitivity to such issues). Unfortunately, those who pay little or no attention to subtypal analysis also tend to demonstrate little or no regard for the changes in the neuropsychological ability structures of children with LD that may transpire during the course of development.

4. Treatment Considerations. Practical experience with children who exhibit marked LD suggests clearly that only some of these individuals respond positively to particular forms of treatment. It is also the case that some forms of treatment for some children with LD are actually counterproductive (Rourke, 1981, 1982). Once again, it is the case that subtypal analysis of children with LD helps to clarify a situation created by the application of the results of contrasting groups methodology. For example, Lyon (1985) has demonstrated that specific subtypes of disabled readers respond very differently to synthetic phonics and "sight-word" approaches to reading instruction. Sweeney and Rourke (1985) also demonstrated what appeared to be an overreliance of phonetically accurate disabled spellers on the phonetic analysis of individual words—to the apparent detriment of their reading speed.

The Idiosyncratic Approach

A strictly individualistic standpoint in this field, although attractive from some clinical perspectives, is viable on neither practical (applied/clinical) nor theoretical grounds. It is patently obvious that persons with LD are unique. It is also the case that most of them can be classified into homogeneous subtypes on the basis of sets of shared relative strengths and deficiencies in neuropsychological skills and abilities. That is, they have enough in common to be grouped (i.e., subtyped) for the purpose of some important aspects of treatment as well as for specific model-testing purposes. The fact that models based upon subtype analysis can, in fact, be shown to be internally consistent and externally (including ecologically) valid (see Rourke, 1985, 1991), suggests strongly that one need not adopt a position that maintains that each and every individual learning-disabled child is so implacably unique that nothing can be said about his or her development, prognosis, and preferred mode of intervention/ treatment. That differential treatment outcomes for different subtypes of children with LD—such as those demonstrated by Lyon and colleagues (Lyon, 1985; Lyon & Flynn, 1991)—obtain is also sufficient proof that strict individualism is not required for treatment efficacy.

In order to accomplish the very desirable goals of scientific and clinical generalizability while insuring the individual applicability of the "general" results of studies in this area, it is necessary to be able to demonstrate that each individual who falls within a particular learning-disability subtype exhibits a very close approximation to the pattern of neuropsychological abilities and deficits that characterizes the subtype as a whole. This should "satisfy" the individualistic criterion, while maintaining the generalizability of treatment and hypothesis-testing imperatives of scientific investigations within this area. The possibility of obtaining this degree of individuation of group results will be particularly apparent when we examine such issues in relationship to the nonverbal learning disabilities subtype.

We turn now to a brief historical overview of the "subtype" approach to the investigation of children with LD.

LD AS A HETEROGENEOUS GROUP OF DISORDERS (SUBTYPES)

Scientific investigation of learning-disability subtypes emerged primarily from careful clinical observations of children who were assessed because they were thought to be experiencing perceptual disabilities and/or LD. Astute observers of children with LD, such as Johnson and Myklebust (1967), noted that there are very clear differences in patterns of assets and deficits exhibited by such children, and that specific variations in developmental demands (e.g., learning to read) appeared to stem from these very different patterns of assets and deficits. In other words, equally impaired *levels* of learning appeared to result from quite different "etiologies," as reflected in different patterns of relative perceptual and cognitive assets and deficits.

The search for subtypes of LD took on added importance when it was inferred that these potentially isolatable patterns of perceptual and cognitive strengths and weaknesses (that were thought to be responsible for LD) might be more or less amenable to different modes of intervention. Indeed, the "subtype by treatment interaction" hypothesis—that is, the notion that the tailoring of specific forms of treatment to the underlying abilities and deficits of children with LD would be advantageous—was alive and well very early in the history of the LD field (e.g., Kirk & McCarthy, 1961). This constituted a second clinical issue that encouraged researchers to seek a determination of subtypal differences among such children. Indeed, many researchers and professionals in the field virtually *assumed* that the matching of intervention/treatment to the underlying strengths and weaknesses of the child who is experiencing outstanding difficulties in learning would be the most efficient and effective therapeutic course to follow.

Positions of this sort were mirrored in the studies conducted by Johnson and Myklebust (1967) and later by Mattis, French, and Rapin (1975). These investigators employed an essentially "clinical" approach to the identification of LD subtypes. This rather important thrust to research, involving as it did an emphasis on subtypal patterns, was accompanied in the late 1970s by that of investigators who sought to isolate reliable subtypes of children with LD through the use of statistical algorithms such as *Q*-type factor analysis and cluster analysis (e.g., Doehring & Hoshko, 1977; Doehring, Hoshko, & Bryans,1979; Fisk & Rourke, 1979; Petrauskas & Rourke, 1979).

At this juncture, it is sufficient to point out that the use of statistical algorithms to assist in the generating of subtypes of learning disabilities is well under way in this decade (e.g., Joschko & Rourke, 1985; Morris, Blashfield, & Satz, 1981). There are clear indications that this type of systematic search for reliable subtypes of children with LD has begun to have a profoundly positive effect on investigative efforts in this area [see Rourke (1985, 1991) for many examples of this]. Furthermore, systematic attempts at establishing the concurrent, predictive, construct, and ecological validity of such subtypes have been proceeding apace (e.g., Fletcher, 1985; Lyon, 1985).

A Systematic Developmental Neuropsychological
Approach to the Study of LD

We turn now to a developmental neuropsychological approach to the study of LD that seeks to understand problems in learning by studying developmental changes in behavior as seen through the perspective of brain-behavior models. It is an approach that combines the study of development of the brain with the study of the development of behavior. This approach involves research strategies that pay as much attention to the development of an individual's approach to material to be learned as they do to (say) the electrophysiological correlates at the level of the cerebral hemispheres that accompany that approach. In a word, it is a systematic attempt to fashion a complete understanding of brain-behavior relationships as these are mirrored in the development of central processing abilities and deficits throughout the life span.

Unfortunately, the utilization of a neuropsychological framework such as this for the investigation of LD in children has often been misinterpreted as reflecting an emphasis on static, intractable (and, therefore, limited) notions of the effects of brain impairment on behavior. Indeed, although specific statements to the contrary have been made on many occasions (e.g., Rourke, 1975, 1978a, 1978b, 1981), many otherwise competent researchers and clinicians persist in the notion that such an approach *assumes* that brain damage, disorder, or dysfunction lies at the basis of LD. Nothing could be further from the truth, since the thrust of much work in this area (see Benton, 1975; Rourke, 1975, 1978a; Taylor & Fletcher, 1983) has been to *demonstrate* whether and to what extent such might be the case.

Be that as it may, the emphasis that we have brought to this enterprise is one that attempts to integrate dimensions of individual and social development on the one hand with relevant central processing features on the other—all of this in order to fashion a useful model with which to study crucial aspects of perceptual, cognitive, and other dimensions of human development. That models and explanatory concepts developed with this aim in mind (e.g., Rourke, 1976b, 1982, 1983, 1987, 1988b, 1989) contain explanations that are thought to apply to some types of children with frank brain damage, to children with LD, and to some aspects of normal human development should come as no surprise, because maximum generalizability is one goal of any scientific model or theory. Specifically with respect to the child with LD, the aspects of these concepts and models that are most relevant are those that have to do with proposed linkages between patterns of central processing abilities and deficits that may predispose a youngster to predictably different patterns of LD that have a significant impact on social as well as academic learning. In addition, these models are designed to encompass developmental change and outcome in patterns of learning and behavioral responsivity.

In the neuropsychology of LD, the important relationships to bear in mind are those that obtain between *patterns* of performance and *models* of developmental brain-behavior relationships. This is not meant to imply something as trite as that LD are the *result* of brain damage or dysfunction. Indeed, the illogical leap that such an implication (assumption) implies is only one of its shortcomings. More important is the fact that, even were such a cause-effect (i.e., brain damage/dysfunction→LD) relationship shown to be the case, it would carry few, if any, corollaries for the understanding of developmental brain-behavior relationships or for their treatment.

The foregoing is not meant to imply that brain-behavior relationships are of little or no importance in the study of LD. Rather, it is simply the case that we currently understand much more about developmental neuro*psychological*-performance interactions than we do about developmental *neuro*psychological-performance interactions. The patterns of interaction among brain, development, and behavior that have, from time to time, been exquisitely hypothesized are, unfortunately, still largely unexplored and must be the subject of rigorous scientific tests (Taylor, 1983).

In subsequent chapters of this work, we examine selected investigations carried out in our laboratory that should serve to illustrate the heuristic properties of this comprehensive developmental neuropsychological framework. The focus of the studies to be discussed in these chapters is the academic and psychosocial dimensions of LD; the perspective employed is one that has emerged from our study of these and related problems over the past quarter of a century in the University of Windsor Laboratory.

To appreciate the main issues involved in this presentation, it is necessary to reflect on the crucial historical issues that bear upon them as well as the relationships that obtain between LD on the one hand and deficits in academic and psychosocial functioning on the other. In this connection, it should be made clear from the outset that the basic hypothesis that we have attempted to test in our work is the following: LD are manifestations of basic neuropsychological deficits; the subtypes of LD in question may lead to problems in academic functioning and/or psychosocial functioning; and, the relationship between neuropsychological deficits,

LD, and academic and social learning deficits can be understood fully only within a changing nature of the academic, socioemotional, and vocational demands with which humans in a particular society are confronted.

To illustrate the research and model development strategy employed in our laboratory that speaks to the issues of concern in this chapter, we turn now to a detailed description of two of the subtypes of children with LD who have been the subject of intensive investigation in the Windsor laboratory.

2

SUBTYPES OF LEARNING DISABILITIES

PATTERNS OF READING, SPELLING, AND ARITHMETIC

A series of studies carried out in the Windsor laboratory over the past few years was designed to determine the neuropsychological significance of patterns of academic achievement. These investigations were stimulated by the unexpected patterns of Wide Range Achievement Test (WRAT; Jastak & Jastak, 1965) Reading, Spelling, and Arithmetic performances that turned up in our examination of the relevance of Verbal IQ (VIQ)-Performance IQ (PIQ) discrepancies in children with LD (Rourke, Dietrich, & Young, 1973; Rourke & Telegdy, 1971; Rourke, Young, & Flewelling, 1971). Specifically, we were interested in determining whether children who exhibit specific patterns of WRAT Reading, Spelling, and Arithmetic performances would also exhibit predictable patterns of neuropsychological abilities and deficits.

STUDY 1: AUDITORY-VERBAL/LINGUISTIC AND VISUAL-SPATIAL-ORGANIZATIONAL ABILITIES

In the first of these investigations (Rourke & Finlayson, 1978), children with LD (defined in a fairly traditional manner: see Rourke, 1975) between the ages of 9 and 14 years were divided into three groups (15 subjects in each group) on the basis of their patterns of performance in reading and spelling tasks relative to their level of performance in arithmetic. The three groups were equated for age and Wechsler Intelligence Scale for Children (WISC; Wechsler, 1949) Full Scale IQ. The subjects in Group 1 were uniformly deficient in reading, spelling, and arithmetic. Group 2 was composed of subjects whose arithmetic performance, although clearly below age expectation, was significantly better than their performances in reading and spelling. The subjects in Group 3 exhibited normal reading and spelling and markedly impaired arithmetic performance. Although *all three groups performed well below age-expectation in arithmetic,* the performances of Groups 2 and 3 were superior to that of Group 1; *Groups 2 and 3 did not differ from one another in their impaired levels of arithmetic performance.* [It should be noted in this context that, in the traditional "contrasting-groups" (Doehring, 1978; Rourke, 1978a) type of study of arithmetic disability, children from Groups 1, 2, and 3 would have "qualified" for admission to the "disabled arithmetic" group. The alarming shortcomings of such a research design are well illustrated by the results of the studies under consideration.]

The three groups' performance on 16 dependent measures, chosen in the light of the results of previous studies in this series (e.g., Rourke et al., 1971), were compared. The results of this investigation may be summarized as follows : (a) the performances of Groups 1 and 2 were superior to those of Group 3 on measures of visual-perceptual and visual-spatial abilities (e.g., WISC Block Design, Target Test), and (b) Group 3 performed at superior levels to Groups 1 and 2 on measures of verbal and auditory-perceptual abilities (e.g., WISC Vocabulary, Speech-Sounds Perception Test). In the context of the results of the previous studies in this series, it was notable that all subjects in Group 1 had a lower VIQ than PIQ, that 14 of the 15 subjects in Group 2 had a lower VIQ than PIQ (one subject had equivalent VIQ and PIQ), and that all subjects in Group 3 had a higher VIQ than PIQ.

It is clear that Groups 1 and 2 performed in a fashion very similar to that expected of groups of older children with learning disabilities who exhibit the WISC High Performance IQ (HP)-Low Verbal IQ (LV) pattern, and that Group 3 performed in a manner expected of older children with LD who exhibit the WISC High Verbal IQ (HV)-Low Performance IQ (LP) pattern (Rourke et al., 1971). It is also important to emphasize that *individual subjects* within the three groups exhibited results on the WISC that were all but indistinguishable from the *group* results reported above. Thus this type of nomothetic research tack did not do violence to any idiosyncratic (ideographic) imperatives, at least in terms of WISC VIQ-PIQ discrepancies.

If there is a reason to believe that WISC VIQ-PIQ discrepancies may be associated with or reflect the differential integrity of information processing systems within the two cerebral hemispheres in older children with LD, as has been suggested (e.g., Rourke, 1975, 1982), then it would appear that the basis on which the groups were chosen in the Rourke and Finlayson (1978) study may also reflect this difference. At the very least, the results of the latter investigation would be consistent with the view that the subjects in Group 3 may be limited in their performance because of compromised functional integrity of systems within the right cerebral hemisphere, and that the subjects in Groups 1 and 2 were suffering from the adverse effects of relatively dysfunctional left-hemispheric systems. These inferences were felt to be reasonable because the subjects in Group 3 did particularly poorly *only* in those skills and abilities ordinarily thought to be subserved primarily by systems within the right cerebral hemisphere, whereas the subjects in Groups 1 and 2 were markedly deficient *only* in those skills and abilities ordinarily thought to be subserved primarily by systems within the left cerebral hemisphere.

Also of importance in the present context was the fact that the two groups of subjects who had been equated for deficient arithmetic performance (Groups 2 and 3) exhibited vastly different performances on verbal and visual-spatial tasks. These differences were clearly related to their *patterns* of reading, spelling, and arithmetic rather than to their *levels of performance* in arithmetic per se. Indeed, although the WRAT Reading, Spelling, and Arithmetic subtest scores of Group 2 were in no case significantly superior to those of Group 3, the performances of Group 2 were significantly superior to those of Group 3 on all of the measures of visual-perceptual and visual-spatial skills employed in this investigation (WISC Picture Completion, Picture Arrangement, Block Design, and Object Assembly; Target Test). More generally, it seemed reasonable to infer that the neuropsychological bases for the impaired arithmetic performances of Groups 2 and 3 differed markedly: Whereas subjects in the Group 2 subtype would appear to experience difficulty in mechanical arithmetic because of "verbal" deficiencies, subjects of the Group 3 subtype would be expected to encounter difficulties with mechanical arithmetic as a direct result of deficiencies in "visual-spatial" abilities. Indeed, a qualitative analysis of the errors made by these two subtypes of youngsters with LD suggested very strongly that this is, in fact, the case (see Strang & Rourke, 1985b, and below).

The methodological implications of such findings for research in children's LD is quite clear: Were subjects from Groups 2 and 3 combined to form a single group defined as "disabled in arithmetic" for the purpose of parametric investigation, comparisons of measures of central tendency between such a combined group and a group performing at a normal level in arithmetic would severely distort and mask the very marked differences in verbal and visual-spatial abilities exhibited by these two LD subtypes. Furthermore, it would appear to be the case that children of these subtypes require quite different modes of educational intervention in order to make academic progress in their areas of deficiency (Rourke, Bakker, Fisk, & Strang, 1983; Rourke & Strang, 1983; Strang & Rourke, 1985b), and should be subjected to "educational validation" study (see Lyon, 1985, and Lyon & Flynn, 1991, for examples of this type of investigation).

STUDY 2: MOTOR, PSYCHOMOTOR, AND SOMATOSENSORY CAPACITIES

Following the Rourke and Finlayson (1978) study, we decided to determine whether these same three groups of 9- to 14-year-old children with LD would differ in predictable ways on tests from a very different neuropsychological domain, namely, those designed to measure motor, psychomotor, and tactile-perceptual skills. In this investigation (Rourke & Strang, 1978), we were particularly interested to determine if any evidence might be adduced to support a view that these groups of children with LD were suffering from differential impairment of functional systems thought to be subserved primarily by structures and systems within the left or the right cerebral hemisphere. We hoped to accomplish this through an analysis of the right- and left-hand performances of these groups of right-handed children with LD children on selected motor, psychomotor, and tactile-perceptual measures.

The motor tests included the Finger Tapping Test and the Strength of Grip Test (Reitan & Davison, 1974). The psychomotor measures included the time measures for the Maze Test (Klove, 1963), the Grooved Pegboard Test (Klove, 1963), and the Tactual Performance Test (Reitan & Davison, 1974). The tests for tactile-perceptual disturbances were those described in Reitan and Davison (1974), as follows: Finger Agnosia, Fingertip Number-Writing Perception, and Coin Recognition. A summary score that included all errors on the latter tests for tactile-perceptual disturbances for each hand was derived for use in the study. The principal results of this investigation and their implications are as follows.

There were no statistically significant differences between or among the groups on the (simple) motor measures over and above those that would be expected to be exhibited by the exclusively right-handed

children employed in this study. The expected superiority of performances for Groups 1 and 2 over those of Group 3 were clearly in
evidence on two of the complex psychomotor measures (Maze and
Grooved Pegboard Tests). Differential hand superiority was found between the groups only on the Tactual Performance Test. Groups 1 and
3 displayed a pattern of poor left-hand performance relative to right-
hand performance on this measure, whereas the exact opposite pattern
was exhibited by Group 2. The left-hand performance of Group 2 was
significantly superior to that of Groups 1 and 3. In line with the patterns
evident for the Maze and Grooved Pegboard Tests, the performances of
Groups 1 and 2 on the "both hands" measure of the Tactual Performance
Test was superior to that of Group 3. Finally, comparisons favoring the
performances of Groups 1 and 2 over those of Group 3 on the composite
tactile-perceptual measure were significant for both the right and left
hands. There was also a tendency evident among subjects in Group 3
for their right-hand performance to be superior to that with the left hand.

Thus it was demonstrated that children with LD in Group 3 have
marked deficiencies relative to Groups 1 and 2 in some psychomotor
and tactile-perceptual skills. In addition, comparisons of these results
with the norms available for these tests (Knights & Norwood, 1980)
indicated that the performances of Group 3 fell well below age expectation on these measures, whereas the performances of Groups 1 and 2
were well within normal limits.

The very marked discrepancy between the performances of Groups 2
and 3 on the Tactual Performance Test would offer clear support for the
hypothesis regarding differential hemispheric integrity for these two
groups that was advanced in connection with the Rourke and Finlayson
(1978) study. Confining our discussion to the performances of Groups
2 and 3 in the two studies under consideration, it is clear that Group 2
scored lower than expected on measures of abilities ordinarily thought
to be subserved primarily by systems within the left cerebral hemisphere,
and much better (in an age-appropriate fashion) on measures of abilities
ordinarily thought to be subserved primarily by right-hemispheric systems; the opposite state of affairs obtained in the case of children with
LD of the Group 3 subtype.

A comparison of the results of the Rourke and Strang (1978) study
with those of Rourke and Finlayson (1978) is especially important in
the case of Group 3. The particular pattern that emerged for this group
is one that is somewhat analogous to that seen in the Gerstmann
syndrome (Benson & Geschwind, 1970; Kinsbourne & Warrington,

1963). That is, the children in Group 3 exhibited the following: outstanding deficiencies in arithmetic (within a context of normal reading and spelling); visual-spatial orientation difficulties, including right-left orientation problems; general psychomotor incoordination, including problems that would fall under the rubric of "dysgraphia"; and impaired tactile-discrimination abilities, including finger agnosia. At the same time, it must be emphasized that the patterning of abilities and deficits exhibited by children in Group 3 would appear to be most compatible with relatively deficient *right*-hemispheric systems rather than with deficient *left*-hemispheric systems as advanced by Benson and Geschwind (1970).

The results of the Rourke and Finlayson (1978) and the Rourke and Strang (1978) investigations would appear to have significant and widespread import for the determination of subtypes of youngsters with LD. Indeed, several groups of investigators have carried out studies that have attested to the reliability and validity of this classification system (e.g., Fletcher, 1985; Loveland, Fletcher, & Bailey, 1990; Mattson, Sheer, & Fletcher, 1992; Share, Moffitt, & Silva, 1988; Siegel & Heaven, 1986; White, Moffitt, & Silva, 1992). Rather than deal with these implications at this juncture, however, it would be instructive to consider the results of the last studies in this series—one dealing with the concept-formation and problem-solving abilities of 9- to 14-year-old Group 2 and 3 children (Strang & Rourke, 1983); two others, with the determination of the verbal, visual-spatial, psychomotor, and tactile-perceptual capacities of 7- to 8-year-old Group 1, 2, and 3 children (Ozols & Rourke, 1988, 1991).

Before proceeding to a discussion of the next investigation in this series, it would be well to point out the reasons for excluding children with Group 1 characteristics from an in-depth analysis in conjunction with this and other studies. Reasons for this exclusion relate to the fact that Group 1 appears to be made up of several discrete subtypes of children with LD (Fisk & Rourke, 1979; Petrauskas & Rourke, 1979).

STUDY 3: NONVERBAL PROBLEM SOLVING, CONCEPT FORMATION, AND HYPOTHESIS TESTING

In this investigation (Strang & Rourke, 1983), 9- to 14-year-old Group 2 and 3 children (15 in each group) were chosen in a fashion virtually identical to that employed in Study 1 and Study 2 just reviewed: That is, the primary criteria for group selection were their patterns of academic performance in reading, spelling, and arithmetic. These groups were equated for age and WISC Full Scale IQ (range: 86 to 114). The dependent measures employed in this study included the number of errors on the six subtests of the Halstead Category Test (Reitan & Davison, 1974) and the total number of errors exhibited on the entire test. The form of the Category Test used for children 9 to 15 years of age includes six subtests and 168 items. The sixth subtest includes only review items from subtests 2, 3, 4, and 5 in a randomly ordered fashion. The Category Test is a relatively complex concept-formation measure involving nonverbal abstract reasoning, hypothesis testing, and the capacity to benefit from positive and negative informational feedback. The most important results of this study were the following.

As predicted, Group 3 scored significantly higher on the Category Test total errors score than did children in Group 2. Furthermore, the level of performance of Group 3 children on this measure was approximately one standard deviation below age expectation (Knights & Norwood, 1980), whereas Group 2 children performed in an age-appropriate manner on it. An analysis of performances on the subtests of the Category Test revealed that the performance of Group 2 was significantly superior to that of Group 3 on the final three subtests (4, 5, and 6). It is notable that subtests 4 and 5 of the Category Test are those that are most complex in terms of their requirements for visual-spatial analysis, and that subtest 6 requires incidental memory for the previously correct solutions. As such, subtest 6 is one measure of the child's capacity to benefit from experience with the task.

These results were expected in view of the previously documented deficiencies exhibited by Group 3 children that we thought would have interfered with the normal development of the higher order cognitive skills presumably tapped by the Category Test. Our reasoning for this assertion was as follows. It would seem highly likely that the majority of children in Group 3 have suffered since birth from the ill effects of their neuropsychological deficiencies (i.e., bilateral tactile-perceptual impairment; bilateral psychomotor impairment; and poorly developed visual-perceptual-organizational abilities). In terms of the theory regarding the development of intellectual functions formulated by Piaget (1954), one would expect that these deficiencies would have a negative effect on the successful acquisition of cognitive skills at later stages. Piaget's description of what he considered to be significant sensorimotor activities serves to highlight the importance of tactile-perceptual, psychomotor, and visual-perceptual-organizational functions for the infant and young child. Because Group 3 children are particularly deficient in these neuropsychological functions (and probably have been so since birth), it would seem highly probable that they have not benefited as much as have most children from the sensorimotor period of development. Furthermore, their cognitive operations, particularly those that are not regulated easily by language functions (e.g., higher order analysis, organization, and synthesis), would also be expected to be deficient.

The essentially intact Category Test performance of Group 2 would suggest strongly that language and thought, as Piaget suggested, are quite distinct. Group 2 youngsters, although deficient in many aspects of linguistic and auditory-perceptual functioning, performed at normal levels on this very complex test of nonverbal concept formation and problem solving. Apart from some difficulties exhibited on subtest 1 (which involves the *reading* of Roman numerals), they performed well within age-expectations on the other subtests. They also exhibited a much better developed capacity to benefit from experience with this task than did the Group 3 children. Finally, they showed considerable capacity to deal effectively and adaptively with the novel problem-solving, hypothesis-testing, and cognitive flexibility requirements of the Category Test.

The fact that there is absolutely no evidence of impairment in tactile-perceptual, visual-spatial-organizational, and psychomotor skills in Group 2 children would suggest that their course through the sensori-motor period of intellectual development described by Piaget (1954) would be expected to have been normal. Even though afflicted with fairly obvious difficulties in the development and elaboration of some important psycholinguistic skills, their development of higher order cognitive processes seems to have proceeded without complication. On the other hand, Group 3 children exhibit signs of significant impairment in tactile-perceptual, visual-spatial-organizational, and psychomotor skills. It may be the case that these constitute the conceptual underpin-nings or "building blocks" for the development of skills involving reasoning (such as mathematics), and that deficiencies in them are responsible for the fact that these children have failed to develop higher order concept-formation and problem-solving abilities to a normal degree. Whether and to what extent the relative failures in conceptual reasoning and related abilities are a direct function of inadequate sensorimotor experience must wait upon the results of further research.

SUMMARY OF MAJOR FINDINGS FOR
GROUP 2 (R-S) AND GROUP 3 (A)

Figure 2.1 is included in order to summarize the major findings of the three studies of 9- to 14-year-old children in Groups 2 and 3 (hereafter referred to as Group R-S and Group A, respectively; Group 1 will be referred to as Group R-S-A) reviewed to this point (See Table 2.1 for a clarification of the designations of these groups in the various studies reviewed to this point.) In Figure 2.1, the T score means are structured in such a way that average performance for the particular age group in question, according to the Knights and Norwood (1980) norms, is represented by $T = 50$, with a standard deviation (SD) of 10. Thus a T score of 60 represents a level of performance that is one SD above the mean, whereas a T score of 40 represents a score that is one SD below the mean for the particular age group. This use of T scores allows direct comparisons to be made among the various tests in a type of profile analysis; this would not be possible if raw scores were used.

As can be seen in Figure 2.1, the deficiencies, relative to age-based norms, exhibited by Group R-S children are virtually confined to the "verbal" and especially the "auditory-perceptual" areas. On the other hand, Group A children exhibit deficiencies in a wide variety of visual-perceptual-organizational, psychomotor, tactile-perceptual, and conceptual areas. (Their relative problems with the Auditory Closure Test and the Sentence Memory Test may be a reflection of their difficulties in dealing with novel tasks [Auditory Closure] and their problems in understanding and utilizing semantic/meaningful content as a memory aid [Sentence Memory], as would be expected in terms of the Rourke, 1982, model.) Some dimensions of the relative discriminant validity of the assets and deficits that distinguish these two subtypes of children with LD have been the subject of recent investigations in our laboratory (e.g., Harnadek & Rourke, in press).

QUALITATIVE ANALYSIS: AN EXAMPLE

To this point, we have examined some studies that address issues associated with the concurrent, predictive, and construct validity of subtypes of children with LD who were chosen on the basis of their patterns of academic performances. Of course, it would be of considerable interest to determine if the conclusions arrived at on the basis of these investigations apply in the individual case. If the generalizations

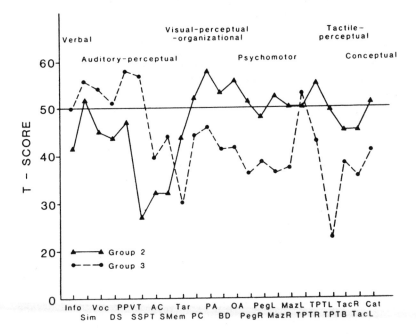

Figure 2.1. Illustration of the Level and Pattern of Performance for Children in Groups R-S and A on a Selection of Neuropsychological Measures

NOTE: Abbreviations: Info, WISC Information subtest; Sim, WISC Similarities subtest; Voc, WISC Vocabulary subtest; DS, WISC Digit Span subtest; PPVT, Peabody Picture Vocabulary Test; SSPT, Speech-Sounds Perception Test; AC, Auditory Closure Test; SMem, Sentence Memory Test; Tar, Target Test; PC, WISC Picture Completion subtest; PA, WISC Picture Arrangement subtest; BD, WISC Block Design subtest; OA, WISC Object Assembly subtest; PegR, Grooved Pegboard Test, right-hand performance; PegL, Grooved Pegboard Test, left-hand performance; MazR, Maze Test, right-hand performance; MazL, Maze Test, left-hand performance; TPTR, Tactual Performance Test, right-hand performance; TPTL, Tactual Performance Test, left-hand performance; TPTB, Tactual Performance Test, both-hands performance; TacR, Composite Score Tactile Perceptual Abilities, right-hand performance; TacL, Composite Score Tactile Perceptual Abilities, left-hand performance; Cat, Halstead Category Test.

derived from empirical studies that compared average performances and variances of Group R-S and Group A children are valid in the individual case, one would expect that a qualitative analysis of the performances of these children would yield a similar pattern of neuro-psychological assets and deficits. The principal requirement in this context is to have at one's avail a sample of behavior/performance that is amenable to componential analysis. The goal would be to determine

TABLE 2.1   A Comparison of the Designations of LD Subtypes Used in
Various Studies

Studies		
Rourke et al. (1971)	Rourke & Finlayson (1978)	
Rourke & Telegdy (1971)	Rourke & Strang (1978)	Rourke (1982, 1987)
Rourke et al. (1973)	Strang & Rourke (1983)	
Group Designations		
Group V = P	Group 1	Group R-S-A
Group HP-LV	Group 2	Group R-S
Group HV-LP	Group 3	Group A

NOTE: Abbreviations: H = high; L = low; V = Verbal IQ; P = Performance IQ
NOTE: The Group designations in each column are those used in the studies at the head of the column. There is a rather close comparability between the pairs of designations in the rows of the middle and last columns (i.e., between Group 1 and Group R-S-A and so on). With regard to the designations in the first and middle columns, Group HP-LV is most like Groups 1 and 2, and Group HV-LP is most like Group 3.

if individuals from each group would reflect these group differences on the tasks involved in such a performance domain.

We have found that mechanical arithmetic performance is a domain that fits the requirements for such analyses. Furthermore, we have determined that systematic qualitative analyses of arithmetic performance do, in fact, reflect these differences and their hypothesized neuropsychological roots, as demonstrated by the following [see Strang & Rourke (1985b) for a more complete treatment of these results].

It should be noted that a child's (or an adult's) errors in arithmetic may vary as a function of such variables as (a) the type of presentation (e.g., written vs. oral), (b) other sources of variability that are inherent in the testing situation itself (e.g., time limits), (c) the type and quality of instruction received in mechanical arithmetic, and (d) age/developmental stage. These dimensions need to be borne in mind when considering the quality of the errors made by children with LD.

When the WRAT arithmetic performances of Group R-S are examined, it is typically found that they make fewer mistakes than is generally the case for children who are deficient in this area. They exhibit a tendency to avoid unfamiliar arithmetic operations or those about which they are uncertain. An exception to this state of affairs is sometimes seen in younger (9- to 10-year-old) children who seem to find ways to calculate correctly without being entirely familiar with the standard procedures (e.g., they may count on their fingers because they do not remember the multiplication tables). The errors made by these children usually reflect some difficulty in remembering mathematical tables or remembering a particular step in the correct procedure for solving a problem. They also tend to avoid problems that require the reading of printed words. Virtually all of the problems that Group R-S children have with mechanical arithmetic can be summarized in terms of the following difficulties: (a) disability in reading, (b) deficiencies in verbal memory, and (c) inexperience with the subject material.

With respect to the latter point, it should be emphasized that it is typical for older Group R-S children to be involved in special education programs in which reading and spelling activities are emphasized. In such programs, attention to the development of mathematical abilities tends to be rather minimal. In any case, it should be clear that the problems that Group R-S children exhibit in the studies described above (i.e., primarily "verbal" in nature) are reflected in a qualitative analysis of their mechanical arithmetic errors. Also reflected in such analyses is their capacity for understanding when problems are too difficult for them and other forms of adaptive behavior that one would expect to see in children whose nonverbal problem-solving, strategy-generating, hypothesis-testing, and informational feedback processing skills are intact.

A qualitative analysis of the mechanical arithmetic errors of Group A reveals a far different picture from that obtaining for Group R-S children. As is the case for Group R-S children, however, the quality of the errors made by Group A children is predictable in terms of their pattern of neuropsychological assets and deficits. Such analyses reveal that they tend to make a large number and a wide range of types of errors on the WRAT Arithmetic subtest. As would be expected, the type and, in some cases, the quality of errors varies somewhat with age. Nevertheless, it is found that some of the oldest children in Group A persist in making the same types of errors as are found in the WRAT profiles of the younger (9-year-old) children in this group. To provide an overview of the most prevalent types of mechanical arithmetic errors that are typically found in the WRAT Arithmetic profiles of Group A children, these have been classified into the seven somewhat overlapping categories below.

1. Spatial Organization. Errors in spatial organization include misaligning numbers in columns (e.g., in a two-digit multiplication question) and any problem that a child might experience with directionality (e.g., subtracting the minuend from the subtrahend in a subtraction question).

2. Visual Detail. Misreading the mathematical sign is an example of an error in visual detail. Failing to include required visual detail in the answer (e.g., a dollar sign or decimal place) may also be classified as a problem related to the appreciation for visual detail.

3. Procedural Errors. In some cases, Group A children miss or add a step to a specific mechanical arithmetic procedure. In other instances, these children may apply a learned rule for one mechanical arithmetic procedure to a dissimilar procedure.

4. Failure to Shift Psychological Set. When two or more operations of one kind (e.g., addition) are followed by an operation of another kind (e.g., subtraction), Group A children sometimes fail to shift set. Instead, they proceed to apply the practiced procedure (addition) to the new operation (subtraction). Other types of procedural errors (see above) can be associated with problems in shifting "psychological set" as well.

5. Graphomotor. Sometimes Group A children write numbers so poorly that they are difficult for the children themselves to read, leading to errors in some questions. The tendency of this group to write with large and rather poorly formed numbers often leads to crowding of work (on the WRAT Arithmetic subtest there is only a fixed amount of space in which to complete each question) and resultant errors. Although graphomotor skills in the case of cursive script (words) tend to become well developed with advancing years, similar advancement in the writing of numbers within calculation procedures is not typical.

6. Memory. In some cases, the Group A child's errors appear to result from his or her failure to remember a particular number fact. It should be noted that this type of error is not predominant in the profiles of Group A children. Often it is clear that the child has the rule available in memory, but fails to access the remembered rule at the point at which it is needed in the arithmetic calculation process. That is, they "forget to remember."

7. Judgment and Reasoning. Children in this group typically attempt questions that are clearly beyond their current realm of expertise. In these cases, they produce solutions that are completely unreasonable in view of the task demands. Unreasonable solutions are also evident on questions for which there is some evidence that the child understands the procedure. In other instances, such children fail to generate a reasonable plan of action when the requirements of a particular mechanical arithmetic question are only slightly different from procedures that the child has obviously mastered. This failure to generalize a particular skill so that it can be adapted to a new, slightly different situation is a predominant feature of the general adaptational characteristics of Group A children.

These aspects of the mechanical arithmetic performance of Group A would appear to be qualitative reflections of (a) their difficulties in visual-spatial-organizational and psychomotor skills and concept-formation and hypothesis-testing abilities, and (b) their adequate verbal memory skills (but with shortcomings in their capacity to deploy such skills adaptively due to difficulties in understanding when particular bits of stored information are needed during the course of a calculation procedure). Some of these types of mechanical arithmetic errors can be found in the profiles of other children with arithmetic impairment who exhibit types and degrees of neuropsychological deficiencies that are somewhat different from those of children in Group A (DeLuca, Rourke, & Del Dotto, 1991). However, many of the foregoing characteristics (especially as regards errors that result from deficient judgment and reasoning) distinguish Group A children from their age-mates with LD whose levels of psychometric intelligence fall within the average range.

STUDY 4: ACADEMIC SUBTYPES
AT AGES 7 AND 8 YEARS

Finally, the results of recent investigations that employed almost all of the aforementioned measures in the investigation of Group 1 (R-S-A), 2 (R-S), and 3 (A) children with LD between the ages of 7 and 8 years (Ozols & Rourke, 1988, 1991) yielded results in the case of verbal, auditory-perceptual, and visual-spatial skills and abilities that were quite comparable with those obtained in the studies of 9- to 14-year-old children (Rourke & Finlayson, 1978). However, as in the Rourke et al. (1973) study of 6- to 8-year-old children who were assigned to groups on the basis of their patterns of WISC VIQ-PIQ discrepancies, the results were not as clear-cut as were those evident for older children with LD, especially in the areas of motor, psychomotor, and tactile-perceptual skills (Rourke & Strang, 1978). In addition, it was not possible to measure higher order (formal) reasoning and concept-formation abilities in an adequate fashion in these younger children, who are, in Piaget's terms, still functioning within the stage of concrete operational thought.

This completes our survey of the levels and configurations of neuropsychological assets and deficits exhibited by subtypes of children with LD who have been classified on the basis of their patterns of academic performances in reading, spelling, and arithmetic. For a summary of validation studies of these subtype comparisons from other laboratories, the interested reader is referred to Fletcher (1985) and Rourke (1991).

COMPARISONS OF GROUP R-S AND GROUP A

Based upon the foregoing analyses, there are several specific conclusions that apply to these two groups. (In the following, "older" refers to 9- to 14-year-old children; "younger," to 7- and 8-year-old children.)

1. Older Group R-S children exhibit some (often no more than mild) deficiencies in the more rote aspects of psycholinguistic skills, such as the recall of information and word definitions; Group A exhibits average to superior skills in these areas.

2. Older Group R-S children exhibit outstanding deficiencies in the more complex semantic-acoustic aspects of psycholinguistic skills such as sentence memory and the auditory analysis of common words. Group A children exhibit less than normal performances in these areas, but their levels of performance are superior to those of Group R-S children. Group A children tend to perform least well on those tests of semantic-acoustic processing that place an emphasis upon the processing of novel, complex, and/or meaningful material.

3. Older Group R-S children exhibit normal levels of performance on visual-spatial-organizational, psychomotor, and tactile-perceptual tasks; Group A children have outstanding difficulties on such tasks. The deficiencies exhibited by Group A children on tactile-perceptual and psychomotor tasks are in evidence bilaterally; when there is evidence of lateralized impairment on such tasks for the Group A child, it is almost always a relative deficiency in performance on the left side of the body. In general, the more novel the visual-spatial, psychomotor,

and tactile-perceptual task, the more impairment, relative to age-based norms, is evident in the Group A child's performance.

4. Older Group R-S children perform normally on nonverbal problem-solving tasks. They have no difficulty in benefiting from experience with such tasks. They are particularly adept at utilizing nonverbal informational feedback in order to modify their performance to meet the demands of such tasks. Group A children exhibit profound problems on nonverbal problem-solving tasks. They give little or no evidence of benefiting from informational feedback and continued experience with such tasks, even when the information provided would be expected to be well within estimates based upon their rote verbal learning capacity (e.g., Verbal IQ).

5. Younger Group R-S children and Group A children exhibit inter- and intragroup patterns of relative assets and deficits on automatic (rote) verbal, semantic-acoustic, and visual-spatial-organizational tasks that are similar to those exhibited by older children in these two groups. The exception is that the more rote aspects of verbal skills tend to be more deficient relative to age-based norms in younger than in older Group R-S children.

6. Differentiations in terms of psychomotor and tactile-perceptual skills and abilities are far less marked in younger than in older children of these two subtypes.

7. Although there is some evidence to suggest that younger Group A children have more difficulty in adapting to novel problem-solving situations than do their Group R-S counterparts, the precise measurement of such suspected difficulties has yet to be completed.

These conclusions and generalizations should be sufficient to make the desired point: Children with LD who are chosen solely on the basis of specific variations in patterns of academic performance (with adequate controls for age, Full Scale IQ, and other important attributes) can be shown to exhibit very different patterns of neuropsychological assets and deficits. In this connection, it should be noted that both of the subtypes under consideration exhibited deficient mechanical arithmetic performance. Thus members of each of these groups could have been included in the "learning-disabled" sample of a contrasting-groups type of study that is designed to compare "arithmetic-disabled" and "normal" children. It should be clear, from the above conclusions and generalizations, that such an "arithmetic-disabled" group could be made up of at least two very distinct arithmetic-disabled subtypes. It is also the case that (a) these subtypes of children share virtually nothing in common, from a neuropsychological standpoint, with each other; (b) their similarly deficient levels of performance in mechanical arithmetic reflect these quite different "etiologies"; and (c) their needs for academic habilitation/rehabilitation with respect to mechanical arithmetic differ markedly from one another (see Rourke, 1983, 1989; Rourke et al., 1983; Rourke, Fisk, & Strang, 1986; Rourke & Strang, 1983; Strang & Rourke, 1985a, 1985b for a discussion of these issues).

DEVELOPMENTAL DYNAMICS OF
GROUP R-S AND GROUP A

An examination of Figures 2.2 and 2.3 will elucidate the models that we have used in our attempts to explain the developmental dynamics of the neuropsychological and adaptive dimensions of these two subtypes of LD. For example, the summaries of the assets and deficits of the Group A subtype (whom we now refer to as the Nonverbal Learning Disabilities [NLD] subtype) should be viewed within a specific context of cause-effect relationships: That is, the Primary neuropsychological assets and deficits are thought to lead to the Secondary neuropsychological assets and deficits, and so on within the four categories of neuropsychological dimensions; and, the foregoing are seen as causative vis-à-vis the academic and socioemotional/adaptive aspects of this subtype. In this sense, the latter dimensions are, essentially, *dependent* variables (i.e., effects rather than causes) in the NLD subtype. The same applies, mutatis mutandis, to the summary of the assets and deficits of the R-S subtype.

Of particular importance for the neuropsychological models developed to account for these and other subtypes of LD in children and for the practicing clinician (Rourke, 1982, 1987, 1988b, 1989), the adaptive implications of the relative abilities and deficits of older Group R-S and Group A children extend well beyond the confines of the academic setting. For example, it is quite clear that Group R-S children tend to fare far better in social situations than do Group A children. More precise delineations of these psychosocial learning considerations are contained in Rourke (1988a, 1989), Rourke and Fuerst (1991), in other recent investigations (e.g., Loveland et al., 1990; Ozols & Rourke, 1985, 1991; Rourke & Fisk, 1992; White et al., 1992), and after a

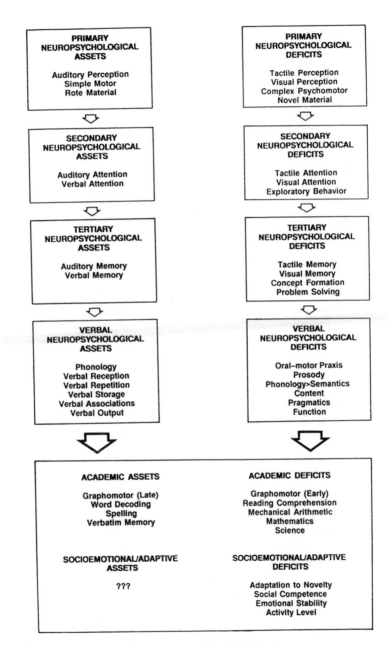

Figure 2.2. Elements and Dynamics of the NLD Syndrome

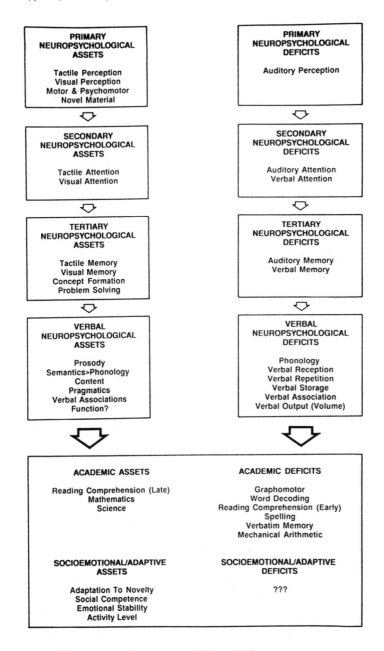

Figure 2.3. Elements and Dynamics of Group R-S

consideration of issues relating to the psychosocial dimensions of LD in Chapter 3.

One very important implication of these views relates to the qualitative analysis of the arithmetic performance of children who exhibit the Group A profile (whom we refer to as children with NLD) that was explained above. When a similar qualitative analysis of the *psychosocial* behavior of children with NLD is carried out, we find that the neuropsychological assets and deficits that appear to lie at the root of their social adaptation deficiencies are virtually identical to those that have a negative impact on their performance in mechanical arithmetic. In a word, the very maladaptive social behavior of children with NLD is seen as stemming from the same neuropsychological deficits as do their problems in arithmetic calculation (e.g., those in visual-perceptual-organizational, psychomotor, and concept-formation skills, and difficulties in dealing with novel problem-solving situations). In the next chapter, we will explore these psychosocial dimensions and their relationship to neuropsychological assets and deficits.

CONCLUSIONS AND GENERALIZATIONS

There are a number of generalizations and conclusions regarding Groups R-S and A (NLD) that can be framed on the basis of the results of the investigations examined in detail above and of others not yet cited. All of these conclusions are inserted at this point so as to provide some structure and closure for what is now known about Group R-S and Group A (NLD). Conclusions 1 through 8 deal with academic and research issues germane to subtyping of LD. Conclusions 7 and 9 are generalizations based upon findings to be discussed in Chapter 3.

1. There are at least two profiles of neuropsychological assets and deficits that can lead to impaired academic learning in older children. The implications of this difference are probably best seen in the case of mechanical arithmetic, where it appears that the consistent differences in performance of these two subtypes imply that there are two quite different sets of neuropsychological assets that are necessary for adequate performance in mechanical arithmetic. Grunau and Low (1987), Miles and Stelmack (in press), and White et al. (1992) have interpreted the results of their studies as in substantial agreement with this position.

2. There is some evidence of a similar set of relationships between these profiles of neuropsychological assets and deficits in younger children, but the reliability and concurrent validity of such findings are not as clear as are those seen in older children.

3. There is evidence of material-specific memory assets and deficits in children with differing patterns of reading and arithmetic disabilities (Brandys & Rourke, 1991; Fletcher, 1985).

4. Subtypes of children with patterns virtually identical to those focused on herein (i.e., subtypes R-S-A, R-S, and A) have been found by other investigators in North America (Fletcher & Satz, 1985; Morris et al., 1986), The Netherlands (van der Vlugt, 1991; van der Vlugt & Satz, 1985), and Finland (Korhonen, 1991). It is especially important to note that children with outstandingly impaired arithmetic relative to reading and spelling—that is, the Group A (NLD) pattern—appear in these large samples of children whose neuropsychological perform-ances have been subjected to statistical subtyping algorithms (primarily cluster analysis).

5. Many investigators in a variety of different laboratories have contributed to the validation of this academic achievement subtype system. These would include investigations by the following: Siegel and Heaven (1986), Loveland et al. (1990), Mattson et al. (1992), Share et al. (1988), Stelmack and Miles (1990), and White et al. (1992).

6. There is evidence that the evoked potentials of children who manifest the Group R-S pattern differ markedly from those who exhibit the Group A (NLD) pattern (Mattson et al., 1992; Stelmack & Miles, 1990). These results are in accord with the Rourke (1982, 1989) models (to be explained below).

7. Different patterns of impaired arithmetic performance vis-à-vis reading and spelling performance are associated with predictable pat-terns of neuropsychological assets and deficits as well as predictable patterns of psychosocial assets and deficits. Evidence in support of this view is found in the following: DeLuca, Rourke, and Del Dotto (1991), Casey, Rourke, and Picard (1991), Fletcher (1985), Fuerst and Rourke (1993), Fuerst, Fisk, and Rourke (1989, 1990), Loveland et al. (1990), White et al. (1992), Ozols and Rourke (1985, 1991), Rourke and Fuerst (1991), Rourke, Young, and Leenaars (1989), and Strang and Rourke (1985a, 1985b). Issues relating to these dimensions of adaptive func-tioning will be explored in the next chapter.

8. The relationships that are seen in the case of "outstandingly poor arithmetic" appear to hold for adults as well as for older children and adolescents (Del Dotto, Fisk, McFadden, & Rourke, 1991; McCue & Goldstein, 1991; Morris & Walter, 1991; Rourke & Fisk, 1992; Rourke, Young, Strang, & Russell, 1986).

9. Methods for the neuropsychological assessment of and intervention with children who exhibit the NLD syndrome as well as other subtypes of children with LD have been developed (Rourke, 1976a, 1981; Rourke et al., 1983; Rourke, Del Dotto, Rourke, & Casey, 1990; Rourke, Fisk, & Strang, 1986). Some of these have been subjected to empirical test (e.g., Williams, Richman, & Yarbrough, 1992). However, there is much that remains to be accomplished with respect to the validation of these modes of assessment and, especially, intervention. These issues will be examined in depth in Chapter 4.

Until now, our focus has been almost exclusively upon one dependent variable: academic functioning. The next important ramification of children's LD to discuss is that of their psychosocial functioning.

ADDENDUM: NLD AND NEUROLOGICAL DISEASE, DISORDER, AND DYSFUNCTION

There is considerable evidence to suggest that outstandingly poor arithmetic performance relative to performance in single-word reading and spelling (i.e., the NLD pattern) is a characteristic of children who exhibit a number of neurological diseases of childhood and a wide variety of developmental disabilities wherein brain impairment is thought to be a principal feature. Examples of this would include hydrocephalus (Fletcher, Francis et al., 1992), myelomeningocele (Wills, Holmbeck, Dillon, & McLone, 1990); traumatic brain injury (Fletcher & Levin, 1988), metachromatic leukodystrophy (Shapiro, Lipton, & Krivit, 1992), callosal agenesis (Casey, Del Dotto, & Rourke, 1990), Williams syndrome (Udwin & Yule, 1991), fetal alcohol syndrome (Streissguth & LaDue, 1987), congenital hypothyroidism (Rovet, 1990), Turner's syndrome (Rovet, 1989, 1993; Rovet & Netley, 1982), velo-cardio-facial syndrome (Golding-Kushner, Weller, & Shprintzen, 1985), insulin dependent diabetes mellitus (Rovet, Ehrlich, Czuchta, & Akler, 1993), adrenal hyperplasia (Nass, Speiser, Heier, Haimes, & New, 1990), Asperger's syndrome (Stevens & Moffitt,

1988), and autism (Szatmari, Tuff, Finlayson, & Bartolucci, 1990). It is also the case that children who have been exposed to very high doses of cranial irradiation for treatment of various forms of cancer exhibit many elements of the NLD syndrome (Fletcher & Copeland, 1988).

What is of crucial importance in this connection is that there are thought to be significant perturbations of white matter development and/or functioning in most of the aforementioned diseases and disabilities. And it is disordered myelinization and/or myelin functioning that has been hypothesized to be the "final common pathway" that eventuates in the NLD syndrome (Rourke, 1987, 1988b, 1989); current and future research will indicate whether and to what extent this is the case. For an example of such efforts, see Fletcher, Bohan et al. (1992).

3

PSYCHOSOCIAL FUNCTIONING OF CHILDREN WITH LD

As in our comprehensive review of the research dealing with this topic (Rourke & Fuerst, 1991), we have organized this chapter around three major hypotheses regarding the relationships between socioemotional functioning and LD that have held sway from time to time over the past 20 years. For each of these hypotheses, we present our characterization of the general and specific conclusions that can be arrived at on the basis of this review. Where appropriate, we highlight the results of studies from our own laboratory that we feel are appropriate to address the issues in question. We also present some clinical observations and generalizations that are felt to flow from the empirical evidence gathered to this point. The presentation closes with some suggestions for future investigations that are needed in order to fill in the gaps of our knowledge in this important area of neurodevelopmental investigation.

HYPOTHESIS 1: SOCIOEMOTIONAL DISTURBANCE CAUSES LD

Before dealing with the two hypotheses that are of particular concern to this presentation, another, widely held position (*Hypothesis 1*) should be outlined and discussed: specifically, the notion that socioemotional disturbance causes LD. In this view, learning problems that children face in school and elsewhere are thought to constitute one reflection of systematic disturbances in socioemotional functioning (e.g., unresolved psychic conflicts). The evidence for this assertion comes from a variety of sources: Some are empirical (e.g., Colbert, Newman, Ney, & Young, 1982), but most are "clinical" in nature (e.g., Brumback & Staton, 1983; Ehrlich, 1983).

38

For example, it has been observed by many whose professional work brings them into contact with youngsters who are experiencing problems in academic achievement that a significant proportion of these children suffer from one or more difficulties of a socioemotional sort: for example, personality conflicts with their teachers that render learning in the classroom difficult, if not impossible; strain associated with difficulties in meeting the (exaggerated) perceived demands of their parents and teachers; extreme psychic conflicts that render them almost incapable of benefiting from ordinary scholastic instruction; "inappropriate" motivation for academic success and social expectancies at variance with those of the school; major psychiatric disorders, such as depression, that remain undiagnosed and/or untreated (Rourke et al., 1983; Rourke, Fisk, & Strang, 1986). These examples illustrate the following: that social conflict between teacher and student should be kept to a minimum if academic learning is to proceed apace; that unrealistic ego-ideals can, and usually do, have a profound negative impact on performance; that significant intrapsychic conflicts or psychiatric disorders, no matter how generated and maintained, can impact significantly on academic performance; and that the school is largely a middle-class institution that requires at least the temporary adoption of its standards (in North America, largely those of the Protestant Ethic) for success in its programs.

These few examples should serve to illustrate the enormous number of complex sets of interactions that can serve to limit significantly the academic progress of untold numbers of students. In all of these instances, the socioemotional "problem" antedates the difficulty in learning; this is so even in the first example cited above. Furthermore, it is assumed that, were the socioemotional problem to be resolved, satisfactory academic performance would ensue. Thus, solving the student-teacher personality conflict, bringing ego-ideals more closely in tune with reality, rectifying the intrapsychic conflict or psychiatric disorder, and leading the student to adopt a motivational posture and social-expectancy set that are more in line with those of the school would be expected to lead eventually to satisfactory academic progress.

That said, it is also necessary to point out that these matters really have to do with academic and other learning difficulties that are not usually included under the rubric of LD. The latter term is commonly reserved for persons whose significant problems in learning are *not* a result of primary emotional disturbance (or mental retardation, primary sensory handicap, inadequate instruction, inappropriate motivation, or cultural/linguistic deprivation—the "exclusionary" criteria embodied in most definitions of LD). Thus although interesting in and of themselves, and of obvious importance for the total understanding and treatment of children's problems in learning, these factors are not properly considered within the context of socioemotional correlates of LD. Hence the remainder of this chapter is devoted to those considerations that fall quite precisely within the latter domain.

HYPOTHESIS 2: LD CAUSE SOCIOEMOTIONAL DISTURBANCE

The first major hypothesis of interest within the present context is one that, as in the aforementioned view, proposes a causal link between learning difficulties and socioemotional disturbance (Rourke & Fisk, 1981). The differences in this instance are that (a) LD, as commonly defined (Rourke, 1975, and above), are the focus of interest; and (b) the causal relationship is reversed: That is, it is proposed that LD lead to disrupted or aberrant psychosocial functioning. This general proposition has a very compelling, tacit appeal for most clinicians; it concretizes a view that is widely held and that has become almost a cornerstone of clinical lore in this area. The reasons for the prima facie appeal of this view are numerous. For example, it appears to make good clinical sense to maintain that a youngster with LD who persists in his or her learning problems throughout the elementary school years will be the butt of criticism and negative evaluations by parents, teachers, and age-mates; that these criticisms will serve to render the child with LD more anxious and less self-assured in learning situations; that a vicious circle will develop that increasingly hampers academic success and encourages progressively more debilitating degrees of anxiety (i.e., learning failure results in increased anxiety, which results in feelings of inferiority, which results in additional learning failure, and so on); that this sort of undesirable situation is virtually inevitable and would be expected to increase in severity as the child fails to make advances in learning.

Research in support of this position has focused on the emotional, social, and behavioral functioning of children with LD, with particular regard to their interpersonal environment. In our comprehensive review of this literature (Rourke & Fuerst, 1991), we examined current research relevant to, or advanced in support of, variants of this general hypothesis. Four specific areas of investigation were scrutinized: (a) patterns of general psychosocial functioning and pathology, (b) social status with respect to peers and teachers, (c) self-concept/self-esteem and attributions, and (d) social competence. Summaries and conclusions regarding the first three of these areas are presented below.

Patterns of General Psychosocial
Functioning and Pathology

Although the results of classroom observation, checklist/rating scale, personality inventory, and longitudinal studies are often contradictory, it would appear that, as a group, children with LD are at somewhat greater than average risk for aberrant psychosocial development or psychopathology. It is also clear, however, that not all children with LD fare poorly in these respects: The range of psychosocial outcomes is probably as great as that seen in any other group of children (i.e., some do very well, some do moderately well, some do poorly, etc.). Although, on average, children with LD may fare worse relative to their normal peers, reliable estimates of the incidence of various degrees and types of disordered psychosocial adaptation have not emerged from the literature. Thus, a simple and clear causal link between LD and psychopathology has not been demonstrated.

Social Status With Respect to Peers and Teachers

The available evidence indicates that, as a group, children with LD may have somewhat lower social status relative to normally achieving peers. This should not be surprising, as research with other groups of children has also shown that, in general, academic achievement and social status are positively (but weakly) correlated (Green, Forehand, Beck, & Vosk, 1980). However, it would appear that only some children with LD have truly low social status and are actively disliked/rejected by peers. On the other hand, some children with LD are quite popular, perhaps because they exhibit attributes that are important to their peers. As in most respects, children with LD are heterogeneous with regard to social status. The nature and extent of relations between peer status and other aspects of psychosocial adaptation are poorly understood, as are other predictors and correlates of social status. Little is known of teacher perceptions and attitudes toward children with LD; however, the available evidence suggests that further investigation of these potentially important issues is warranted.

Self-Concept/Self-Esteem and Attributions

There is some evidence that some children with LD do demonstrate reduced self-concept with respect to academic and, perhaps, intellectual domains. However, the evidence that children with LD have lower self-concept/self-esteem either globally or in other specific domains is not convincing. There is no evidence that children with LD demonstrate a particular pattern of attributions with respect to success or failure in academic and other settings (Bender, 1987). Thus there is no convincing evidence that, in children with LD, reduced self-concept is related to attributions and locus of control. There is no compelling evidence that (a) children with LD demonstrate a pattern of attributions and behaviors consistent with a condition of learned helplessness, (b) self-concept and attribution patterns of LD children are adversely affected by experience of failure, and (c) self-concept and attribution patterns are related to aberrant behavior in children with LD.

The conclusions of the research that appears to have established a causal link between LD and patterns of psychosocial dysfunction may seem fairly straightforward and unambiguous. There are, however, a number of serious flaws in most of the investigations that have led to them. Some of the major shortcomings of this research are as follows.

METHODOLOGICAL AND THEORETICAL CONSIDERATIONS

The research reviewed above that relates to the interpersonal environments of children with LD has not been terribly contributory. The results of many studies are trivial, contradictory to one another, and not supported in replication attempts. There is little to suggest that the factors identified as "characteristic" of children with LD in these studies are related to one another in any meaningful fashion. In sum, the evidence regarding socioemotional functioning that emerges from this research is, at best, equivocal. A coherent and meaningful pattern of personality characteristics (including psychopathology, problems with self-concept/self-esteem, attributions and locus of control, social status, and so on) of children with LD does not emerge from this literature. This may very well be the case because such an univocal pattern does not obtain. At this juncture, it would be well to point out some of the more obvious methodological inadequacies of this research.

Definition of LD. There was no consistent formulation of the criteria for LD in these studies. For example, some employed vague or undefined groups, whereas others used the ratings of teachers and other school personnel that remain otherwise unspecified. It is obvious that this lack of clarity and consistency had a negative impact on the generalizability of such findings. Clear, consensually validatable definitions are vital in this area of investigation.

Measurement of Maladjustment. "Emotional disturbance," "socio-emotional adjustment," "behavior disorder," "antisocial behavior," and other constructs of psychosocial functioning have been operationalized at least as inadequately as have LD in many of these studies. It is clear that the use of reliable and valid psychometric instruments would be preferable to the largely subjective nature of the judgments of these crucial dependent variables that has characterized much of this research.

Developmental Considerations. Several studies offer support for the notion that the nature of the skill and ability deficits of (some subtypes of) children with LD varies with age (e.g., McKinney et al., 1985; Morris et al., 1986; Ozols & Rourke, 1988; Rourke, Dietrich, & Young, 1973). Because it would seem reasonable to infer that the psychosocial functioning of (some subtypes of) children with LD would also vary as a function of age (considered as one index of developmental change), the aforementioned inconsistencies in research results may reflect differences in the ages of the subjects employed. To investigate this possibility, cross-sectional or longitudinal studies, such as those carried out by Spreen (1988) and colleagues, are necessary.

Heterogeneity. Virtually all of the studies upon which the conclusions stated above were based have employed a research design that involves comparisons of undifferentiated groups of children with LD to equally undifferentiated groups of normal achievers. This approach, which aims to identify the particular pattern of socioemotional disturbance characteristic of children with LD, tends to obscure within-group differences. As Applebee (1971) has pointed out, employment of this comparative-populations approach can be justified only if one can safely assume that children and adolescents with LD are homogeneous in terms of their abilities and deficits.

Homogeneity of psychosocial functioning, or the lack thereof, has become an increasingly important topic of investigation in recent years. Although some investigators have previously noted that not all children with LD behave in a similar manner in the psychosocial domain, discussion of this issue has been largely confined to brief, post hoc descriptions. These descriptions are often couched as explanations for unexpected or contradictory findings, rather than as a proper subject of investigation. Research into the neuropsychological aspects of LD, however, has suggested strongly that: (a) children with LD constitute a markedly heterogeneous population in terms of their skills and abilities, and (b) meaningful subtypes of children with LD can be identified in a reliable fashion using a variety of methods (e.g., Fletcher, 1985; Morris et al., 1981; Rourke & Finlayson, 1978; Rourke & Strang, 1978; Strang & Rourke, 1983).

Apart from our continuing work at the University of Windsor, presented in detail in the next section, relatively few systematic attempts to develop a psychosocial typology of children with LD have been reported in the literature. Notable exceptions to this generalization are the work of Loveland et al. (1990), McConaughy and Ritter (1986), and, to a lesser extent, Silver and Young (1985).

Even more disturbing than this paucity of relevant research is the apparent disregard for its potential relevance that is reflected in even very recent publications. For example, Vaughn, Zaragoza, Hogan, and Walker (1993) followed 30 students—10 each grouped as undifferentiated LD, "low achievers" (LA), and "average/high achievement" (A/HA)—over a 4-year period (Kindergarten to Grade 3) to determine their relative incidence of social skills and behavior problems. They concluded that LD and LA children did not differ from one another in these domains, but that both demonstrated more behavior problems and lower social skills than did the A/HA students. In addition to extremely small sample sizes, dubious group membership criteria for distinguishing LD and LA children (e.g., the LA children, unlike the LD children, had not been referred for special education programs), and grossly inappropriate generalizations from marginally significant differences (i.e., with considerable overlap) between the groups, the researchers seemed blithely unaware of the subtype literature, much less prepared to deal with its implications. Unfortunately, unless and until more rigorous criteria for group selection are adopted in this field, journal pages are very likely to continue to be filled with "research" of this sort that replicates the outlandish mistakes of the past.

Lack of a Conceptual Model. In the vast majority of the studies that we have reviewed, there was an obvious absence of a conceptual model to guide the research efforts in question. This was especially the case in the area of social competence. A notable exception to this generalization is the formulation of Wiener (1980). For example, at the very minimum, a componential analysis of social competence should sensitize the researcher to the possibility that, whereas some subtypes of children with LD may experience social competence problems because they lack certain perceptual, cognitive, or behavioral skills, others may manifest such problems as a more direct result of attitudinal/motivational difficulties. It should also be clear that different patterns of perceptual, cognitive, and behavioral skills and abilities may encourage different types or degrees of socially incompetent behavior.

MODEL DEVELOPMENT: AN EXAMPLE

The results of one study from our laboratory (Ozols & Rourke, 1985) can be used to illustrate our hypothesis testing/model development approach to the determination of the psychosocial ramifications of these two subtypes of LD. In this study, the performances of two groups of children with LD, one exhibiting a pattern of relatively poor auditory-perceptual and language-related skills within a context of well-developed visual-spatial-organizational skills (similar to Group R-S), the second exhibiting the opposite pattern of abilities and deficits (similar to Group A), were compared on four exploratory measures of social judgment and responsiveness. As predicted on the basis of the Rourke (1982) model, one result of this study revealed that children in the language-disorder group performed more effectively than did those in the visual-spatial disorder group on tasks requiring nonverbal responses; in contrast, tasks requiring verbal responses yielded exactly the opposite results. These results suggest that social awareness and responsiveness vary markedly for these two subtypes of children with LD, probably as a result of an interaction between their particular patterns of central processing abilities and deficits and the specific task demands of the four measures employed. A recent study by Loveland et al. (1990) has replicated and extended these findings.

The results of the Ozols and Rourke (1985) study should be viewed within the context of a study by Ackerman and Howes (1986). In the latter study, it was demonstrated that, although social competence deficits often occur in many children with LD, it is the case that some children with LD do not exhibit such deficits and are seen as popular with their peers and active in after-school interests. These findings, taken together, would suggest that a study designed along the lines of the Porter and Rourke (1985) investigation (to be described below) may reveal an analogous set of "social competence" subtypes (i.e., some "normal" and others "disturbed" in terms of social competence). (The studies by McKinney & Speece, 1986, and Speece, McKinney, & Apelbaum, 1985, contain some data that could be used to address this question directly.) It is clear that, as in the case of the investigation of emotional disturbance in youngsters with LD, the examination of their social competence should eschew the homogeneous, contrasting-groups methodology that has heretofore characterized all but a few studies in the field in favor of one that does justice to the heterogeneity of subtypes evident in the LD population.

Furthermore, it would appear to be the case that efforts to relate patterns of abilities and deficits on the one hand and components of social competence on the other may generate much more interesting data and conclusions than do approaches that simply search for correlates of LD (considered as a univocal phenomenon) and either emotional disturbance or problems in social competence. The studies reviewed in connection with the examination of *Hypothesis 3* constitute another step beyond the latter type of simplistic contrasting-groups/unitary deficit methodologies.

THE WINDSOR TAXONOMIC RESEARCH

Before turning our attention to the most recent formulations of the psychosocial functioning of children with LD (so-called *Hypothesis 3* approaches) we examine in detail one issue raised in the previous section: heterogeneity.

In our laboratory we have undertaken a research program with the immediate aim of more precisely describing the psychosocial functioning of children with LD. In these studies, we have applied multivariate statistical subtyping methods, such as Q-factor analysis and some of the many variants of cluster analysis, to selected scales of the Personality Inventory for Children (PIC; Wirt, Lachar, Klinedinst, & Seat, 1977, 1984), in an attempt to derive both reliable and valid psychosocial subtypes of children with LD. These studies are the initial steps in a comprehensive research program aimed at the development of a psychosocial typology of children with LD; we refer to them as the "Windsor Taxonomic Research." Note that, in this section of our presentation, we concentrate on describing the characteristics and reliability of the typology that has emerged from this research. Other aspects of these studies are more germane to issues raised in connection with *Hypothesis 3* approaches (see below).

The results of five of our studies (Fuerst et al., 1989, 1990; Fuerst & Rourke, 1993, under review; Porter & Rourke, 1985) are summarized schematically in Figure 3.1. Each box on the chart represents a subtype derived from the source noted in the left-most column of the figure. Within each box is a descriptive label that characterizes the mean PIC profile of the subtype and, in the lower right corner, the relative size of the subtype expressed as a percentage of the subjects classified within the study. Correlations between corresponding subtypes across studies appear on the connecting lines. Note that although some of the subtypes are arranged hierarchically, this order is based on the temporal course of our research and is not meant to imply that such a hierarchical division does, in fact, exist. Whether certain broad categories of psychosocial functioning can be usefully and accurately divided into subcategories, as implied by Figure 3.1, can only be determined by further research.

The first four rows of the figure present the subtypes found in the first four studies (Porter & Rourke, 1985; Fuerst et al., 1989; Fuerst et al., 1990; and Fuerst & Rourke, 1993; respectively). The fifth row (Overall) summarizes the typology that emerged across those four studies. In this case, the relative size values represent the average percentage of subjects assigned to a subtype across the four studies. The final four rows of the figure present the results from Fuerst and Rourke (1993). The results of that study are broken down into Young "cluster-analysis-derived" (CAD) subtypes, Middle CAD subtypes, Old CAD subtypes, and "profile-matching-derived" (PMD) subtypes based on the entire sample. In this portion of the figure, the correlations on connecting lines represent the correlation between the mean PIC profile of the subtype and the corresponding prototype developed from Studies 1-4.

Internal Validity (Reliability) of the Typology

Ideally, subtyping methods of any type should produce reliable, homogeneous groups that can be replicated across different samples and classification techniques (Everitt, 1980). This issue is of particular

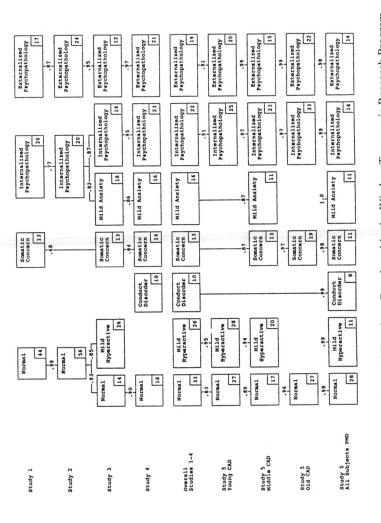

Figure 3.1. Summary of the Psychosocial Typology Developed in the Windsor Taxonomic Research Program

NOTE: Study 1 refers to Porter and Rourke (1985); Study 2 refers to Fuerst, Fisk, and Rourke (1989); Study 3 refers to Fuerst, Fisk, and Rourke (1990); Study 4 refers to Fuerst and Rourke (1993); Study 5 refers to Fuerst and Rourke (1993). See text for further explanation.

concern when multivariate subtyping techniques are applied in an exploratory fashion to data with relatively unknown statistical properties. Multivariate subtyping techniques, such as cluster analysis and Q-factor analysis, will always produce some grouping of cases, even if purely random data are used in the procedures, and different statistical subtyping techniques can, and often do, produce disparate solutions when applied to the same data. Replicability of solutions across different samples from the same population, and across different subtyping techniques, is a crucial step in determining the validity of the subtypes so derived (Fletcher, 1985). When the results of our five studies are considered, it is apparent that four of the subtypes (i.e., Normal, including Mild Hyperactive; Somatic Concern; Internalized Psychopathology, including Mild Anxiety; Externalized Psychopathology) are readily replicable using different samples, statistical techniques, and sets of PIC scales. The reliability of the conduct disorder subtype is currently unknown.

Description of the Typology

Note that in Figure 3.1 correlation coefficients (calculated between the mean PIC profiles of the subtypes) were used to match up corresponding subtypes across the five studies. Overall, across the Studies 1 to 5, seven distinct subtypes (viz., Normal, Mild Hyperactive, Mild Anxiety, Somatic Concern, Conduct Disorder, Internalized Psychopathology, and Externalized Psychopathology) have been identified. By averaging the PIC scores of corresponding subtypes across studies (e.g., PIC scores of all of the Normal subtypes) it is possible to obtain "prototypical" mean PIC profiles for the seven subtypes. Prototypical profiles are presented in Figures 3.2 through 3.8.

Of course, presentation of PIC profiles without interpretation does not describe behavior, as the scale labels are, in some respects, arbitrary. For example, elevation of the Psychosis scale above 70 T does not mark a child as psychotic. Similarly, the labels given to the subtypes, such as Normal or Mild Hyperactive, were used more as descriptions of the pattern of scores on the mean PIC profiles than as descriptions of behavior. For example, the PIC profile of the Normal subtype is, in fact, abnormal, with clinically meaningful elevations on some PIC scales. However, elevations on the Academic Achievement, Intellectual Screening, and Development scales in the context of an otherwise roughly flat profile are unremarkable, or *normal*, in samples of children with LD.

(Continued on page 57)

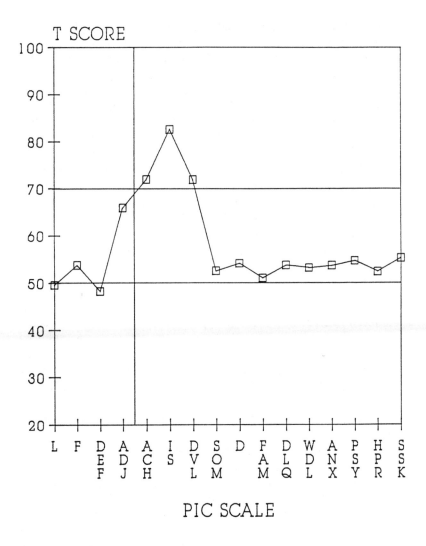

Figure 3.2. PIC Profile for the Normal Prototype

NOTE: Abbreviations: L, Lie; F, Frequency; DEF, Defensiveness; ADJ, Adjustment; ACH, Achievement; IS, Intellectual Screening; DVL, Development; SOM, Somatic Concern; D, Depression; FAM, Family Relations; DLQ, Delinquency; WDL, Withdrawal; ANX, Anxiety; PSY, Psychosis; HPR, Hyperactivity; SSK, Social Skills.

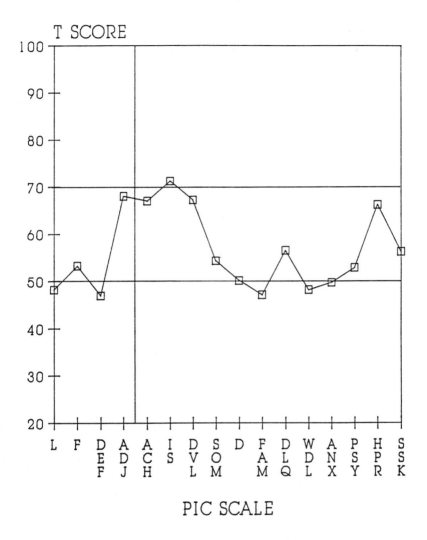

Figure 3.3. PIC Profile for the Mild Hyperactive Prototype

NOTE: Abbreviations: L, Lie; F, Frequency; DEF, Defensiveness; ADJ, Adjustment; ACH, Achievement; IS, Intellectual Screening; DVL, Development; SOM, Somatic Concern; D, Depression; FAM, Family Relations; DLQ, Delinquency; WDL, Withdrawal; ANX, Anxiety; PSY, Psychosis; HPR, Hyperactivity; SSK, Social Skills.

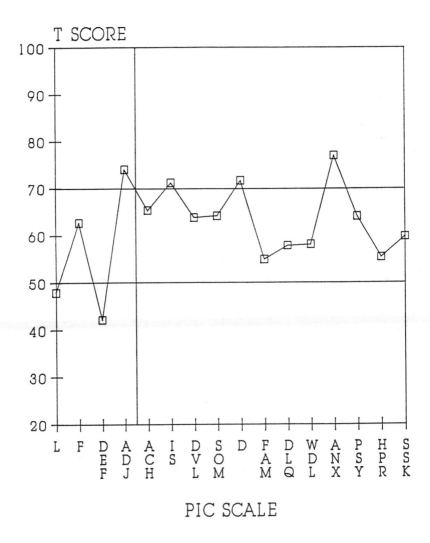

Figure 3.4. PIC Profile for the Mild Anxiety Prototype

NOTE: Abbreviations: L, Lie; F, Frequency; DEF, Defensiveness; ADJ, Adjustment; ACH, Achievement; IS, Intellectual Screening; DVL, Development; SOM, Somatic Concern; D, Depression; FAM, Family Relations; DLQ, Delinquency; WDL, Withdrawal; ANX, Anxiety; PSY, Psychosis; HPR, Hyperactivity; SSK, Social Skills.

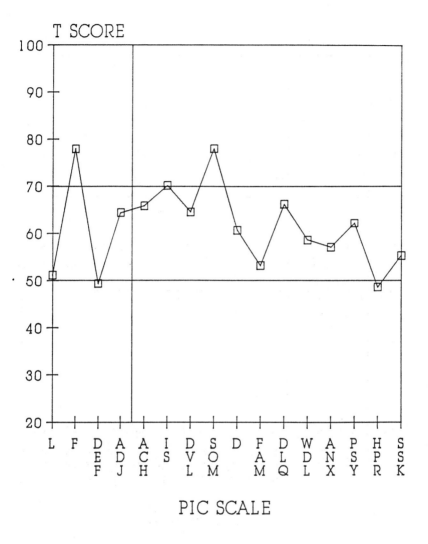

Figure 3.5. PIC Profile for the Somatic Concern Prototype

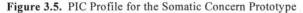

NOTE: Abbreviations: L, Lie; F, Frequency; DEF, Defensiveness; ADJ, Adjustment; ACH, Achievement; IS, Intellectual Screening; DVL, Development; SOM, Somatic Concern; D, Depression; FAM, Family Relations; DLQ, Delinquency; WDL, Withdrawal; ANX, Anxiety; PSY, Psychosis; HPR, Hyperactivity; SSK, Social Skills.

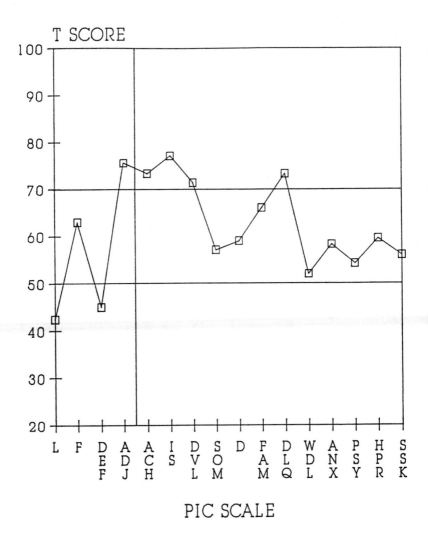

Figure 3.6. PIC Profile for the Conduct Disorder Prototype

NOTE: Abbreviations: L, Lie; F, Frequency; DEF, Defensiveness; ADJ, Adjustment; ACH, Achievement; IS, Intellectual Screening; DVL, Development; SOM, Somatic Concern; D, Depression; FAM, Family Relations; DLQ, Delinquency; WDL, Withdrawal; ANX, Anxiety; PSY, Psychosis; HPR, Hyperactivity; SSK, Social Skills.

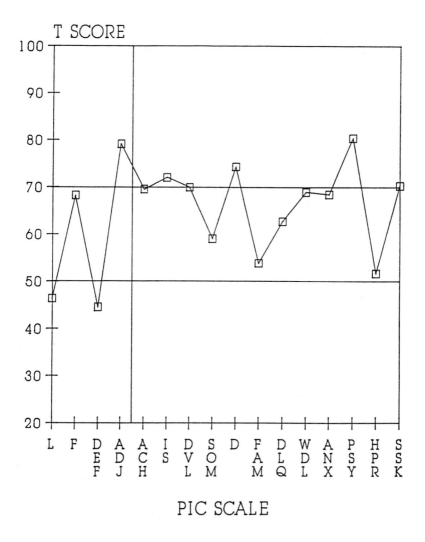

Figure 3.7. PIC Profile for the Internalized Psychopathology Prototype

NOTE: Abbreviations: L, Lie; DEF, F, Frequency; Defensiveness; ADJ, Adjustment; ACH, Achievement; IS, Intellectual Screening; DVL, Development; SOM, Somatic Concern; D, Depression; FAM, Family Relations; DLQ, Delinquency; WDL, Withdrawal; ANX, Anxiety; PSY, Psychosis; HPR, Hyperactivity; SSK, Social Skills.

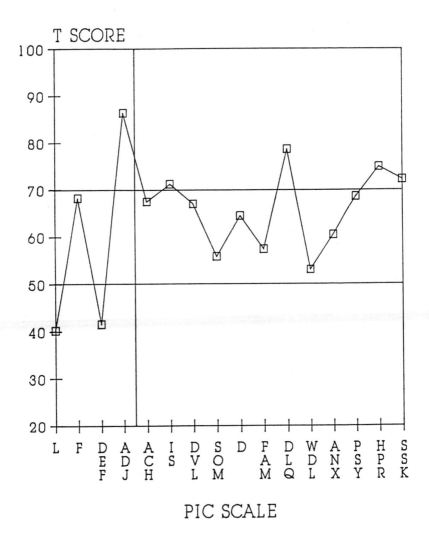

Figure 3.8. PIC Profile for the Externalized Psychopathology Prototype

NOTE: Abbreviations: L, Lie; F, Frequency; DEF, Defensiveness; ADJ, Adjustment; ACH, Achievement; IS, Intellectual Screening; DVL, Development; SOM, Somatic Concern; D, Depression; FAM, Family Relations; DLQ, Delinquency; WDL, Withdrawal; ANX, Anxiety; PSY, Psychosis; HPR, Hyperactivity; SSK, Social Skills.

In this section, the subtypes are discussed in terms of psychosocial adaptation, or general patterns of behavioral function/dysfunction that would be expected based on our current understanding of the PIC. Note that these characterizations are actually *expectations* or predictions that, in the process of establishing the external validity of the typology, must be tested in future research.

Two of the subtypes have mean PIC profiles that suggest relatively good psychosocial functioning. The profile of the Normal subtype (Figure 3.2) shows mean elevations above 70 *T* on the Achievement, Intellectual Screening, and Development scales (the so-called cognitive triad; a pattern found, to a greater or lesser extent, in all subtypes), and a very flat profile on all other clinical scales. The caretakers of these children are most concerned with cognitive development and academic performance. The mean PIC profile of the Somatic Concern subtype (Figure 3.5) is similar to that of the Normal subtype, but it is marked by elevation of the Somatic Concern scale. The caretakers of these children are likely to express distress about their child's physical well-being and health. Physical complaints could span a wide range of difficulties, including visual problems, dizziness, headaches, syncope, fatigue, and gastrointestinal dysfunction. It should be noted, however, that, as with other psychosocial measures tapping somatic domains, it is not possible to determine the degree to which such complaints might be "functional," rather than "organic," in nature on the basis of the PIC profile. Elevation of this scale may be indicative of a need for medical assessment and intervention rather than reflective of psychosocial dysfunction.

Two of the subtypes evidence modest degrees of psychosocial dysfunction. Children in the Mild Hyperactive subtype (Figure 3.3) show a relatively unremarkable PIC profile that is distinguished by a single significant elevation above 70 *T* on the Intellectual Screening scale and a somewhat higher than usual mean score on the Hyperactivity scale. This suggests fairly good psychosocial adaptation in most domains, as in the Normal subtype, with the possibility of rather mild acting-out behaviors. The profile of the Mild Anxiety subtype (Figure 3.4) suggests significant psychosocial disturbance, with notable, but relatively modest, peaks on the Intellectual Screening, Depression, and Anxiety scales. Overall, this profile suggests symptoms of mild anxiety and depression and is somewhat reminiscent of the PIC profile of the Internalized Psychopathology subtype.

In some respects, the PIC profile of the Conduct Disorder subtype (Figure 3.6) also suggests modest psychosocial dysfunction, with a single peak on the Delinquency scale. The behaviors that may be demonstrated by such children, however, are likely to be more problematic for caretakers and peers than are those demonstrated by children in the Mild Hyperactive or Mild Anxiety subtypes. Children with this profile may show insensitivity toward others, a disregard for rules and limits, impulsivity, and hostility. Truly delinquent behavior, such as verbal and physical aggression, destructiveness, lying, and stealing, may be exhibited by some children.

The mean PIC profile of the Internalized Psychopathology subtype (Figure 3.7) displays prominent elevations on a number of subscales that suggest significant, internalized, socioemotional difficulties. This profile includes high scores on the Adjustment, Depression, Withdrawal, Anxiety, and Psychosis scales, with moderate, though clinically relevant, elevations on Achievement, Development, and Social Skills scales. Children in the Internalized Psychopathology subtype are likely to be depressed, anxious, and emotionally labile. Inappropriate affect, difficulties with cognition and orientation to reality, and social isolation have been associated with this profile. Social interaction and general interpersonal functioning may present serious problems for these children.

The mean PIC profile of the Externalized Psychopathology subtype (Figure 3.8) is also elevated on a number of scales. Children in this subtype have particularly high mean scores on the Adjustment, Delinquency, Hyperactivity, and Social Skills scales. This profile also suggests significant behavioral disturbance; however, unlike the Internalized Psychopathology subtype, these children are apt to exhibit hyperkinetic, acting-out types of behavior. Such children may be hostile, impulsive, restless, and emotionally unstable, and have low frustration tolerance. Aggressive, violent, and destructive behavior may also be part of the clinical picture.

RELATIONS BETWEEN AGE
AND PSYCHOSOCIAL FUNCTIONING

Of the five studies discussed above, the relations between age and patterns of psychosocial functioning were directly examined only in Fuerst and Rourke (1989). In this study, we examined the relations between age and patterns of psychosocial functioning in children with LD. To this end, we constructed a sample of 728 children with LD between the ages of 7 and 13 years. For some analyses, the children were subdivided into three age levels: "Young" (7 to 8 years old; 201

subjects), "Middle" (9 to 10 years; 258 subjects), and "Old" (11 to 13 years; 269 subjects). As in the first four studies, psychosocial functioning was defined by subtypes derived from PIC scores. Two methods were used to derive the subtypes.

The first method employed k-means cluster analysis, applied separately to each of the young, middle, and old samples. The resulting k-means partitions were validated by replication, using a variety of hierarchical-agglomerative clustering techniques. The subtypes (referred to as "cluster-analysis-derived" [CAD] subtypes) at each of the three age levels were very similar and were strongly related to clusters found in our previous studies. At each age level, roughly the same number of subtypes were found (four, six, and four subtypes at Young, Middle, and Old age levels, respectively), which suggests that with increasing age children with LD do not show greater diversity of psychosocial functioning. Also, at all three age levels, Normal, Internalized Psychopathology, and Externalized Psychopathology subtypes were found, which suggests that major *patterns* of psychosocial functioning are consistent across ages 7 through 13. Finally, the Internalized Psychopathology and Externalized Psychopathology CAD subtypes were very similar across the young, middle, and old samples. It thus appears that with increased age there is no change in the *level* of pathology evidenced by children in frankly maladjusted subtypes.

The second classification method used in this study involved assigning subjects to the subtypes of the typology derived in previous research on the basis of similarity of PIC profile shape. As outlined above, and summarized in Figure 3.1, previous research in our laboratory has produced a typology of seven psychosocial subtypes (viz., Normal, Somatic Concern, Mild Anxiety, Mild Hyperactive, Conduct Disorder, Internalized Psychopathology, and Externalized Psychopathology). Calculating the mean PIC scores on all 16 scales for the seven previously derived subtypes resulted in the creation of "prototypical" PIC profiles for those subtypes. Correlations between each subject's PIC profile and the seven prototypical PIC profiles were calculated, and subjects were assigned ("matched") to the subtypes to which their PIC profiles correlated most strongly. When the subtypes formed by this profile matching technique ("profile-matching-derived" [PMD] subtypes) were further broken down at the young, middle, and old age levels, there were no differences between the resulting mean PIC profiles in terms of either profile shape or elevation within each subtype. Furthermore, the distribution of subjects across the subtypes was comparable at each of the three age levels. Again, these results demonstrated that children with LD show similar patterns of psychosocial functioning, and similar forms and levels of psychopathology, from ages 7 to 13 years.

Considering the results of the Fuerst and Rourke (1993) study, it is clear that there is remarkable stability in patterns of psychosocial adaptation of children with LD across the elementary school years. No evidence was found to support the notion that children with LD are likely to develop more serious types or degrees of psychopathology as they grow older. Similarly, the results of the Fuerst and Rourke (1993) study indicate that, given a particular pattern of psychosocial adaptation, there is no substantial change in level of adaptation with increasing age. Thus, overall, as children with LD grow older, they show no increased risk for the development of pathological patterns of psychosocial adaptation, nor do they show any deterioration in level of psychosocial functioning.

These results are very much at variance with *Hypothesis 2* formulations of the psychosocial functioning of children with LD. Recall that such formulations generally hold that the negative consequences of having a learning disability (such as frustration, anxiety, or peer rejection due to continued academic failure, or a discrete cognitive deficit that perpetually disrupts psychosocial functioning) in time produce maladjustment by grinding down the child's adaptive capacity in some fashion. Although cumulative negative experiences may be deleterious to some children with LD, the results of Fuerst and Rourke (1993) and others (e.g., Chapman, 1988; Chapman & Boersma, 1980; Jorm, Share, Matthews, & Maclean, 1986; and Strang, 1981) suggest strongly that this is not generally the case. It is clear that some children with LD evidence significant maladjustment (e.g., the Internalized Psychopathology and Externalized Psychopathology subtypes); however, the development of pathological patterns of functioning is not more likely with increasing age, nor is deterioration in level of adaptation.

This conclusion must, of course, be tempered by the same consideration that motivated the studies reviewed in this section: heterogeneity. Just as some children with LD will not fall neatly within the typology presented above (to the chagrin of statistically oriented researchers, outliers *do* have the annoying habit of showing up in the clinic waiting room), experience dictates that some children with LD demonstrate abnormal psychosocial development. However, this series of studies suggests that, when such changes are observed in clinical settings, factors other than simple increased age and cumulative exposure to negative experiences must be considered. An example of a specific, well-delineated subpopulation of children with LD that *does* show abnormal psychosocial development with advancing age, and the factors that may cause or contribute to this process, will be presented in a subsequent section of this chapter.

General Conclusions

The results of the foregoing studies conducted in our laboratory constitute a formidable, perhaps irrefutable, challenge to the view that children with LD are relatively uniform in terms of their socioemotional functioning. Furthermore, these studies cast doubt on the notion that LD, broadly considered, constitute a sufficient condition for the production of emotional disturbance. The results of these studies suggest strongly that some children who meet commonly accepted definitions of LD show signs of significant socioemotional disturbance, whereas others do not; on balance, it appears that most do not. The important question at this juncture becomes one of determining whether there is a set of characteristics that differentiates: (a) children with LD who develop adaptive socioemotional functioning from those children who develop maladaptive socioemotional functioning (i.e., presence or absence of psychopathology, and/or level of psychopathology), and (b) children with LD who develop particular patterns of psychosocial functioning (i.e., type of pathology, such as internalized vs. externalized). This issue is discussed in greater detail in the following section, wherein relations between neuropsychological skill/ability patterns and socioemotional disturbance are examined.

HYPOTHESIS 3: SPECIFIC PATTERNS OF CENTRAL PROCESSING ASSETS AND DEFICITS CAUSE SPECIFIC MANIFESTATIONS (SUBTYPES) OF LD AND SPECIFIC FORMS OF SOCIOEMOTIONAL DISTURBANCE

The second major hypothesis that has been investigated in this area is one that proposes a causal connection between particular patterns of central processing abilities and deficits on the one hand and particular subtypes of both LD and socioemotional functioning on the other (Rourke & Fisk, 1981). In other words, the academic and behavioral adaptation of children with LD are not seen as directly related (except in a correlational sense) as in *Hypothesis 2* approaches, but are instead

primarily determined by neurocognitive or neuropsychological assets
and deficits.

This formulation of the interrelations between LD and psychosocial
functioning is relatively new. Unfortunately, some of the research in
this area has been of less than stellar quality (see Weller & Strawser,
1987, for a brief review of relevant studies). A rather extreme example
is found in a study by Stellern, Marlowe, Jacobs, and Cossairt (1985),
in which they attempted to relate hemispheric cognitive modes (or
styles) to academic performance, classroom behavior, and emotional
disturbance in a sample of behaviorally disordered and normal control
children. Cognitive style (i.e., left hemisphere preferred, right hemisphere preferred, or integrated) was assessed by means of a paper-and-
pencil self-report scale. Briefly, Stellern et al. (1985) found that
emotional disturbance was weakly associated with a right hemisphere
cognitive mode. In addition to poor subject selection procedures, unso-
phisticated and questionable statistical methods, and the use of an
unvalidated measurement instrument, the entire premise of left versus
right hemisphere cognitive modes reveals a rather limited and largely
erroneous view of brain-behavior relations.

A marginally better study is one by Glosser and Koppell (1987). In
this investigation, the authors divided 67 children with learning problems (so identified by referral sources with no other criteria used) into
left hemisphere impaired, right hemisphere impaired, or nonlateralized
impairment. Unfortunately, the classification scheme used was only
vaguely described by the authors and appeared to have been developed
more to provide adequate coverage when the sample was partitioned
than on a rational or empirical basis. The three groups were compared
on scores derived from behavioral checklists created by the investigators. Overall, children showing left hemisphere impairment (as judged
by the authors) tended to show more evidence of depression and anxiety,
whereas children showing right hemisphere impairment tended to have
more somatic complaints. Those children with nonlateralized impairment tended to show more distractibility, motor activity, and aggression. Roughly comparable results have been reported by Nussbaum and
Bigler (1986), who found that children with putative left hemisphere
impairment (judged on the basis of measures of psychometric intelligence and academic achievement) showed somewhat greater levels of
personality and behavioral deviance.

More recently, Nussbaum et al. (1988) administered a battery of
neuropsychological tests to 219 children, from 7 to 12 years old,

referred for testing because of learning problems. The investigators developed composite "anterior" and "posterior" cortical impairment scores based on neuropsychological measures used in the assessment. On the basis of these composite scores they classified 33 subjects into either anterior or posterior impairment groups. These two groups were then compared on Child Behavior Checklist (Achenbach & Edelbrock, 1983) and PIC (Wirt et al., 1984) measures completed by parents. The results showed that the anterior impairment group exhibited more evidence of social withdrawal, aggression, hyperactivity, and externalizing pathology, whereas the posterior impairment group showed somewhat greater levels of anxiety.

Although these and other studies fall within the framework of *Hypothesis 3* investigations, they clearly represent little or no improvement over many of the *Hypothesis 2* investigations reviewed above, for much the same methodological reasons (poor or absent definitions of LD, poor operationalization of psychological constructs, questionable classification procedures, etc.). Disregard of developmental considerations is also of particular concern in these investigations.

In our view, the central importance of developmental considerations in this area cannot be overemphasized. Unfortunately, there is a tendency in some studies to assume that brain-behavior relations derived from research with adults can be extrapolated without modification to children with LD: for example, that a particular test that may have some value for localization of dysfunction in adults with demonstrated cerebral insult necessarily has similar significance across all age ranges and populations. As Rourke et al. (1983) have pointed out, there are numerous reasons (e.g., rapid maturation of the nervous system, loss of existing ability vs. failed acquisition of ability, abnormal or atypical development) why generalizations of adult models of cerebral functioning to children must be done with extreme caution and be subject to careful empirical testing. Similarly, in some studies there is a tendency to frame research problems within static models of limited scope (or, worse still, to present entirely atheoretic investigations). Research undertaken within a limited or trivial theoretical framework tends to produce limited or trivial results. Recent reviews and theoretical papers by Spreen (1989) and Rourke (1988a) have emphasized the need to consider both the components and the dynamics of neurologic, cognitive, academic, and psychosocial development and adaptation when developing models to account for the socioemotional difficulties faced by children with LD. Although this is clearly a monumental task, choosing to ignore complexity when formulating research questions does not make a phenomenon under investigation simpler.

A more sophisticated test of *Hypothesis 3* involves an examination of the results of several LD subtype investigations aimed at the determination of patterns of central processing abilities and deficits that characterize such subtypes, and the patterns of socioemotional responsivity that appear to be related to them. We turn now to a review of studies carried out in our laboratory that have focused on the psychosocial functioning of subtypes of children and adolescents with LD. These studies have their origins in the discovery of the neuropsychological dimensions of the Group R-S and Group A children, and they have followed a course best described as an attempt to develop a nomological net and the exploitation of a form of the multitrait-multimethod approach to validity (Cook & Campbell, 1979). Furthermore, they were designed specifically to test hypotheses derived from neurodevelopment models: Rourke (1982) in the earlier studies; Rourke (1987, 1988b, 1989) in the later studies.

Strang and Rourke (1985a):
Patterns of Psychosocial Functioning
of Subtypes R-S and A (NLD)

When the average PIC profiles of children chosen to approximate the characteristics of these two subtypes of learning-disabled children were compared (Strang & Rourke, 1985a), it was clear that the profile for Group A was similar to that exhibited by the "emotionally disturbed" (internalized psychopathology) group in the Porter and Rourke (1985) and Fuerst et al. (1989) studies, whereas the profile for Group R-S children was virtually identical to that exhibited by the "normal" group in those studies. Additional examination of three factor scores derived from the PIC revealed that Groups R-S and A did not differ significantly on the "concern over academic achievement" factor, but that they differed sharply on the factors of "personality deviance" and "internalized psychopathology." In both of the latter cases, the Group A levels of deviation were significantly higher (i.e., more pathological) than were those for Group R-S.

These two sets of results, taken together, offer strong support for *Hypothesis 3*: namely, that particular patterns of central processing abilities can eventuate in (a) markedly different subtypes of LD and academic functioning (Groups R-S and A) and (b) markedly different patterns of socioemotional functioning (one characterized by normalcy; the other, by an internalized form of psychopathology and personality deviance). Because such group results can be deceiving when applied to the individual case, it should be emphasized that there was very little variance evident in the PIC protocols of the children classified into Groups R-S and A in these studies. Furthermore, the interested reader may wish to consult case studies of such youngsters in three recent works (Rourke, 1989, 1991; Rourke et al., 1983; Rourke & Fisk, 1992; Rourke, Fisk, & Strang, 1986) for evidence of such consistent differences in socioemotional manifestations.

The Fuerst et al. (1990) and Fuerst and Rourke (1993) investigations (reviewed above) also attempted to address *Hypothesis 3* considerations. In these studies, however, we took the opposite approach to that employed in the Strang and Rourke (1985a) investigation, in that we first attempted to develop a psychosocial typology (using the PIC and statistical methods), and then examined the manner in which these subtypes differed on cognitive and academic measures.

Fuerst, Fisk, and Rourke (1990):
Patterns of WISC VIQ-PIQ
Discrepancies and Psychosocial Functioning

In this study, the subjects were selected so as to comprise three (equal-sized) groups with distinctly different patterns of WISC (Wechsler, 1949, 1974) Verbal and Performance IQ scores. One group had VIQ greater than PIQ by at least 10 points (VIQ > PIQ), a second had VIQ less than PIQ by at least 10 points (VIQ < PIQ), and a third had VIQ-PIQ scores within 9 points of each other. As discussed above (see *The Windsor Taxonomic Research*), the application of several cluster analytic techniques yielded an apparently reliable solution suggesting the presence of six distinct personality subtypes. The frequencies of the three VIQ-PIQ groups within each of these psychosocial subtypes were calculated and compared.

We found that, within the Normal subtype, children with VIQ > PIQ occurred at a much lower frequency (roughly 6% of the subtype) than did either children with the opposite pattern of discrepancy (VIQ < PIQ), or those with no significant difference between VIQ and PIQ. This was also the case in the Mild Anxiety subtype, in which subjects with VIQ > PIQ were found at a rate significantly below expectation (about 5% of the subtype). In the Mild Hyperactivity subtype, the frequencies of subjects from the three VIQ-PIQ groups were approximately equal. These results indicated that, overall, within normal and mildly disturbed subtypes of children with LD, there was a tendency for VIQ > PIQ children to occur at lower frequencies than do VIQ = PIQ or VIQ < PIQ children. There were only about half as many VIQ > PIQ children in these three groups as there were VIQ = PIQ or VIQ < PIQ children.

In the Internalized Psychopathology subtype, subjects with VIQ = PIQ were found at significantly lower than expected frequencies (about 15% of the subtype). On the other hand, subjects with VIQ > PIQ were found at a higher frequency than would be expected (roughly 46% of the subtype), and at a higher frequency than VIQ < PIQ subjects (39%). Within the Externalized Psychopathology subtype, subjects with VIQ > PIQ were found at a much higher frequency (about 63% of the group) than were children with either VIQ = PIQ or VIQ < PIQ. Thus, unlike the normal and mildly disturbed groups, within subtypes showing severe psychosocial disturbance there was a strong tendency for VIQ > PIQ subjects to be found at higher frequencies than either the VIQ = PIQ or VIQ < PIQ subjects. In total there were about twice as many VIQ > PIQ children in these two "severe" groups as there were VIQ = PIQ or VIQ < PIQ children.

Fuerst and Rourke (1993):
Patterns of WRAT Reading, Spelling,
and Arithmetic and Psychosocial Functioning

In this investigation, six personality subtypes were also generated (see *The Windsor Taxonomic Research,* above). With one exception, these were the same subtypes as those found in the Fuerst et al. (1990) study. The differences between these six subtypes on WRAT Reading, Spelling, and Arithmetic standard scores were examined. Overall the six subtypes were indiscriminable on WRAT Arithmetic. However, there were significant differences between some of the subtypes on WRAT Reading and Spelling. The Externalized and Internalized Psychopathology subtypes had mean WRAT Reading scores that were significantly higher than those of the Normal and Somatic Concern subtypes. Similarly, the Externalized and Internalized Psychopathology subtypes scored higher on WRAT Spelling than did the Conduct Disorder and Normal subtypes, and the Internalized Psychopathology group also scored higher than did the Somatic Concern subtype.

These findings were echoed when WRAT Reading, Spelling, and Arithmetic were considered simultaneously in a canonical discriminant analysis. The first canonical function was significant, providing better than chance discrimination between the groups. When the standardized scoring coefficients for this function were considered, it was apparent that scores on this variable were, in fact, essentially simple sums of WRAT Reading and Spelling scores, with Arithmetic playing a trivial role. Examination of group means on the canonical variables indicated that the Normal, Somatic Concern, and Conduct Disorder groups were indistinguishable on this variable. These three groups were, however, clearly separated from the higher scoring Externalized and Internalized Psychopathology Groups, which appeared to form a second "clump" on their own. The Mild Anxiety group fell about midway between these two sets of subtypes.

These results suggest that children referred for neuropsychological assessment (mostly because of suspected LD) with relatively well-developed reading and spelling skills (but with deficient mechanical arithmetic skills) are more likely to appear in PIC subtypes with profiles suggestive of severe psychopathology, be it of the internalizing or externalizing type. On the other hand, children with relatively mild somatization or conduct disorder problems are indistinguishable from normal children on the basis of these reading and spelling skills. Children with symptoms of mild anxiety and depression appear to fall between these two extremes and cannot be distinguished from either on the basis of these skills.

Fuerst and Rourke (1993) also compared the subtypes on WRAT Reading minus Arithmetic (RA) and Spelling minus Arithmetic (SA) scores. Overall the Internalized Psychopathology group had not only the largest absolute difference on RA and SA, but also showed deficient Arithmetic relative to both Reading and Spelling (i.e., a pattern identical to that shown by the Group A subtype in previous studies). The other subtypes showed much smaller discrepancies on RA and SA, and, in some instances, discrepancies in the opposite direction (e.g., the Normal, Somatic Concern, and Conduct Disorder subtypes had Arithmetic scores that were *higher* than their Spelling scores). This contrast (Internalized Psychopathology vs. all other subtypes) was statistically significant. None of the other subtypes could be differentiated from one another on the basis of these measures.

Related Developmental Studies

Two investigations that were designed to determine the developmental outcome for Group A children are also useful for evaluating *Hypothesis 3*. Rourke, Young et al. (1986) compared the performances of Group A children and a group of clinic-referred adults on a wide variety of neuropsychological variables. The adults presented with VIQ-PIQ discrepancies and WRAT patterns that were virtually identical to the analogous patterns in Group A children. It was demonstrated that the patterns of age-related performances of the adults and the children on the neuropsychological variables were remarkably similar. In addition, the adults were characterized by internalized forms of psychopathology that bore a striking resemblance to those exhibited by Group A youngsters. In a related study, Del Dotto, Rourke, McFadden, and Fisk (1987) confirmed the stability of the neuropsychological and personality characteristics of this subtype of LD over time.

IMPLICATIONS OF HYPOTHESIS 3 STUDIES

Although the results of these studies are quite straightforward, the patterns of relations revealed by them, and their implications for the current discussion, are fairly complex and require detailed explanation.

1. Strang and Rourke (1985a) demonstrated that Group A subjects (good reading and spelling performance relative to arithmetic) evidence greater, clinically significant, psychopathology as compared to Group R-S subjects (poor reading and spelling relative to arithmetic). Fuerst and Rourke (1993) also demonstrated that children evidencing severe psychopathology tend to perform better in reading and spelling relative to children with normal psychosocial functioning or relatively benign psychosocial problems. Both the Strang and Rourke (1985a) and Fuerst and Rourke (1993) studies also revealed that children showing a Group A pattern of academic performance tend to evidence a particular *type* of psychopathology (internalized). Thus, there is a relationship between patterns of academic functioning and patterns of psychosocial functioning (both level and type of pathology) in at least one subtype of children with LD.

2. It is difficult to argue that patterns of academic performance (i.e., good reading and spelling relative to arithmetic, or vice versa) influence psychosocial functioning. That is, there is no obvious explanation for

the observation that Group A children evidence greater psychopathology as compared to Group R-S children. Similarly, it is also difficult to argue that different patterns of psychosocial functioning can directly produce different patterns of academic achievement. (An exception to this assertion might be cases of primary psychopathology, such as major depressive disorder or attention deficit disorder. As explained in the *Hypothesis 1* section above, these cases lie outside the realm of LD.)

3. Considering Point 2, it is logical to propose that there is a third factor accounting for the apparent relationship between patterns of academic functioning and psychosocial functioning. Though it is certainly possible that there could be many different factors producing this apparent relationship, a single factor would provide the most parsimonious explanation.

4. The most likely candidate for this intervening factor is cognitive functioning. Previous research has clearly indicated that patterns of academic functioning are strongly related to patterns of cognitive functioning, as measured by neuropsychological/psychometric instruments. These measures include—but are by no means limited to—WISC VIQ-PIQ discrepancies (Rourke, Dietrich, & Young, 1973; Rourke & Finlayson, 1978; Rourke & Telegdy, 1971; Rourke et al., 1971). The logical direction of causation in this relationship is that cognitive factors influence academic performance.

5. The results of Fuerst et al. (1990) have demonstrated that patterns of cognitive functioning, measured by WISC VIQ-PIQ discrepancy, are associated with psychosocial functioning. Specifically, children showing the pattern of WISC VIQ > PIQ tend to be found in subtypes demonstrating severe psychopathology, whereas children with VIQ = PIQ or VIQ < PIQ tend to be found in subtypes with normal or mildly disturbed psychosocial functioning. As before, it is difficult to conceive of patterns of psychosocial functioning as causative with respect to patterns of cognitive functioning (with the exceptions noted in Point 2 above). It is more logical to propose that patterns of cognitive functioning influence psychosocial functioning.

6. It thus follows that cognitive/neuropsychological functioning may, at one and the same time, influence academic performance on the one hand and psychosocial functioning on the other. Patterns of cognitive/neuropsychological functioning may be the intervening factors accounting for the apparent relationship between academic performance and socioemotional adjustment. However, further investigation,

using more direct and detailed measures of cognitive/neuropsychological functioning, is required in order to have greater confidence in this conclusion.

PSYCHOSOCIAL DYNAMICS
IN GROUPS R-S AND A (NLD)

It would appear that children who exhibit the Group A (NLD) profile of neuropsychological abilities and deficits are likely to be described by parents as emotionally or behaviorally disturbed. In contrast, Group R-S children (with outstanding difficulties in many aspects of psycholinguistic functioning) are so described at much lower frequencies. More generally, it may be that the pattern of NLD described approximates a sufficient condition for the development of some sort of socioemotional disturbance (Rourke, 1987, 1989), whereas the pattern of central processing abilities and deficits exhibited by the subtype of psycholinguistically impaired child examined in this series of studies may not constitute the same sufficient basis for such an outcome.

This is not meant to imply that children characterized by the Group R-S pattern—which we have come to characterize as the Basic Phonological Processing Disorder subtype (see Rourke, 1989, and Chapter 5 of this work)—will never experience socioemotional disturbance. Indeed, clinical experience (e.g., Rourke et al., 1983; Rourke, Fisk, & Strang, 1986) suggests that many do. Rather, these results suggest that, for the Group R-S subtype, factors in addition to psycholinguistic deficiency may be necessary for disturbed socioemotional functioning to occur. Such "additional" factors may include some of those mentioned in connection with the emotional disturbance-learning problem relationship outlined in the initial (*Hypothesis 1*) section of this review (e.g., teacher-pupil personality conflicts, unrealistic demands by parents and teachers, inappropriate motivation and social expectancies). Others would appear to include the presence of salient antisocial models, selective reinforcement of nonadaptive and socially inappropriate behaviors, and any number of other factors that have the potential for encouraging problems in the socioemotional functioning of even normally achieving youngsters.

At this point, it would be well to cite a number of broad, general conclusions that appear warranted on the basis of the results of the intensive investigations of LD subtypes in our own and others' laboratories that have been carried out over the past two decades. These include generalizations that relate to academic performance as well as to psychosocial/adaptive functioning.

CONCLUSIONS AND GENERALIZATIONS

With respect to the role of subtyping pursuits in the field of LD, it would appear that the following conclusions and generalizations are warranted:

1. There is no single, unitary pattern of neuropsychological abilities and deficits displayed by children with LD. Indeed, distinct subtypes of LD have been isolated in a reliable fashion in a number of studies.

2. There is an emerging body of evidence attesting to the content, concurrent, predictive, construct, and clinical validity of some subtypes of learning-disabled youngsters (e.g., Casey, Rourke, & Picard, 1991; Rourke, 1991a, 1991b, 1991c).

3. There is no single, unitary pattern of personality characteristics, psychosocial adaptation, social competence, self-concept, locus of control, or other facet of socioemotional functioning that we have examined that is characteristic of all children with LD (Porter & Rourke, 1985; Fuerst et al., 1989, 1990; Rourke, 1988a). For a fuller discussion of these issues and for a review of the studies that support this conclusion and those spread in numbers 4 through 11 below, see Rourke and Fuerst (1991).

4. Some children with LD experience mild to severe disturbance of socioemotional functioning. However, most children with LD appear to achieve adequate psychosocial adaptation.

5. There are distinct types of socioemotional disturbance and behavior disorder that may be displayed by children with LD. These various manifestations of emotional and behavioral disorder may be more frequent among children with LD than among their normally achieving peers; our knowledge about the precise types and incidence of emotional and behavioral problems in children with LD is gradually emerging.

6. There is one pattern of central processing abilities and deficits (nonverbal learning disabilities; NLD) that appears to lead to the following: a particular configuration of academic achievement (well-developed word-recognition and spelling as compared to significantly

poorer mechanical arithmetic), increased risk of psychopathology, and a tendency to develop an internalized form of socioemotional disturbance. Other patterns of central processing abilities and deficits (those marked by outstanding difficulties in psycholinguistic skills) appear to lead to particular patterns of academic achievement (striking problems in reading and spelling, and varying levels of performance in mechanical arithmetic), with some correlative effect upon the incidence of psychopathology but with no particular effect upon its specific manifestations.

7. There is no conclusive evidence that children with LD are prone to developing problems with substance abuse, truly antisocial behavior, or delinquency. Carefully conducted longitudinal research suggests that, as a group, children with LD are no more likely to develop these problems than are normal children.

8. There is no conclusive evidence that children with LD, as a group, tend to become more prone to socioemotional disturbance with advancing age relative to normally achieving peers.

9. One exception to Point 8 is the worsening in the manifestations of psychopathology and the increasing discrepancies between abilities and deficits that are exhibited by children and adolescents of the NLD subtype. This is the case in spite of the fact that the *pattern* of neuropsychological abilities and deficits and the specific manifestations of psychopathology in such individuals remain quite stable over time.

10. Developmental differences in the manifestations of LD appear to obtain for some subtypes of LD. For example (see number 9 above), there appears to be a worsening of the manifestations of psychopathology and the increasing discrepancies between abilities and deficits exhibited by children with NLD.

11. It would appear that at least one subtype of learning disability (i.e., NLD) is evident within groups of children who are suffering from various types of neurological disease, disorder, and dysfunction. This should encourage the search for reliable patterns of central processing abilities and deficits among other groups that are typically excluded from such scrutiny (e.g., the mentally retarded).

12. Efforts to clarify the relationships between learning disabilities and patterns of neuropsychological abilities and deficits should eschew the "contrasting-groups/unitary deficit" approach in favor of research efforts that deal adequately with the heterogeneity of the LD population, both with respect to their patterns of abilities and deficits and with

respect to their distinctive forms and manifestations of psychopathology. Model developments (e.g., Fletcher & Taylor, 1984; Rourke, 1982, 1987, 1988b, 1989) must be sufficiently complex and sophisticated to encompass and illuminate these heterogeneous patterns of central processing abilities/disabilities among children with LD. Continuing to carry out essentially atheoretical, correlational studies of matched groups of learning-disabled and normally achieving children to address the important theoretical and clinical issues in this area is counterproductive.

We turn now to a consideration of the clinical (i.e., the assessment and intervention) dimensions that we have found useful in the delivery of services to children who exhibit LD.

4

ASSESSMENT AND INTERVENTION

NEUROPSYCHOLOGICAL ASSESSMENT PROCEDURES FOR CHILDREN WITH LD

Content and Rationale

Extensive treatments of the neuropsychological assessment procedures that we have found useful for children and adolescents can be found in Rourke (1976a, 1981), Rourke et al. (1983, especially chap. 5), and Rourke, Fisk, and Strang (1986, especially chaps. 1 & 2). Several of the most important dimensions of this exercise are emphasized below.

Comprehensiveness. A neuropsychological assessment of a child who is thought to have LD should be comprehensive in nature. Our experience with procedures that aim simply to "screen" for LD is that they typically do more harm than good. Even disregarding for the moment the very high levels of false positives and false negatives that such procedures typically generate, it should be pointed out that it is rarely, if ever, useful to know simply that a child does or does not have LD. In fact, such knowledge, especially when a positive "diagnosis" of LD is made on the basis of such an assessment procedure, may very well be counterproductive for the child. This is so because there are patterns of assets and deficits evident in various subtypes of children with LD that differ very markedly from one another (see, e.g., Figures 2.2 and 2.3 for a comparison of the NLD and R-S profiles). Thus lumping them under the common rubric of LD may lead to gross misunderstanding on the part of professionals and other caretakers involved with the child, not to mention the potentially dramatic negative ramifications that such a homogeneous designation might have for treatment.

In addition, it is usually essential to know at least as much about what a child with LD *can* do as it is to know what he or she *cannot* do, if one's goal is to design an appropriate treatment/intervention plan for the youngster. A designation of LD very often accentuates the disabilities and deficits that the child exhibits while virtually ignoring the assets and strengths that are probably going to be useful in compensatory intervention strategies. Most treatment plans for children with LD usually involve a combination of direct "attack" on the deficits and the exploitation of the child's assets for compensatory modes of adaptation. In general the older and the more impaired the child, the more likely it is that compensatory techniques accentuating the use of the child's assets will be found to be effective and will tend to dominate the treatment picture. Comprehensive neuropsychological assessment procedures are designed with this "accentuate the positive" rule in mind.

But, what constitutes a comprehensive assessment? As explained in detail in the works cited above, a comprehensive neuropsychological assessment is one that involves the measurement of the principal skills and abilities that are thought to be subserved by the brain. Thus a fairly broad sampling of tasks involving sensory, perceptual, motor/psychomotor, attentional, mnestic, linguistic, and concept-formation/problem-solving/hypothesis-testing would need to be administered. In addition, it would be well to vary the levels of complexity of such tasks (from quite simple to quite complex), and to present tasks that vary along the dimensions of rote and novel requirements. Inclusion of tasks that vary from those that involve information processing within a single modality to those that involve the coordination and execution of response requirements within several modalities would also be desirable. It is clear that the aforementioned continua of tests and measures are not mutually exclusive. Finally, it is often important in the analysis of children with LD to have available fairly comprehensive personality and "behavioral" data on the child. Standardized tests of important dimensions of psychopathology, activity level, and common problem behaviors are often useful—sometimes essential—for this purpose.

A collection of tests and measures that includes these dimensions would meet the minimal requirements for comprehensiveness. For a list of the tests that fulfill such criteria and that we use routinely in our evaluation of children referred for neuropsychological assessment, the interested reader should examine the Appendix section of Rourke et al.

(1983) or Rourke, Fisk, and Strang (1986). Some specification of these procedures is contained within the next section of this chapter.

Standardized Administration Procedures and the Availability of Norms. We have found that testing procedures that are standardized and that have norms available for them are quite essential in the study of children who exhibit LD and any number of other neuropsychological difficulties. This is so for a variety of reasons, not the least of which is the fact that the manifestations of LD may change in many ways over time; the predictability that can be seen to obtain in such circumstances is best couched in terms of deviations from age-expected performances that either decline, remain stable, or increase over time. For example, without the availability of developmental norms and standardized tests, it would not have been possible to determine the predictable developmental manifestations of the NLD syndrome. Furthermore, the use of unstandardized procedures would have made it all but impossible to assess its fulminations, responses to therapy, and other aspects of its course in the individual patient. In the last analysis, standardized assessment procedures and their attendant benefits are what makes it possible to translate clinical lore into rigorous, testable clinical generalizations (e.g., the NLD syndrome and model).

Procedures That Are Amenable to a Variety of Methods of Inference. The methods of inference for comprehensive neuropsychological assessment procedures first proposed by Reitan (1966) are as important now as they were when he articulated them. It is quite crucial that one (a) be able to apply *level of performance* interpretations (especially within the context of developmental norms as outlined above), (b) have a sufficiently broad sample of performances so that *pathognomonic signs* of brain impairment may emerge, (c) have data in a variety of realms that are amenable to the *differential score* approach, and (d) be able to carry out systematic *comparisons of performance on the two sides of the body.* In the analysis of the NLD and other LD subtypes, all of these methods of inference are employed, as the data spread in the previous sections dealing with hypothesized subtypes illustrates.

There are a number of other features of comprehensive, systematic neuropsychological assessment that are important considerations in the analysis of the behavior of children with LD. Some of these will arise in the next section. More comprehensive treatments of such issues are contained in the works cited above.

A DEVELOPMENTAL NEUROPSYCHOLOGICAL
REMEDIATION/HABILITATION MODEL

Figure 4.1 contains a modification of a remediation/habilitation model that was developed by Rourke et al. (1983) and Rourke, Fisk, and Strang (1986) for general neuropsychological assessment. It is modified slightly in Figure 4.1 to take into consideration the special dimensions of LD. Note that the model is couched in terms of "steps." In explaining the content and dynamics of the model, we will consider each step in order.

Step 1: Impact of LD on Academic and Social Learning

This step appears, at first blush, quite simple. It is, however, meant to imply a number of dimensions that are fairly complex and sometimes difficult to determine in the assessment process. In general, the pictorial representation of this step is meant to imply that the levels and patterns of neuropsychological assets and deficits that constitute the child's LD may have a differential impact on the child's capacities for academic and social learning. The impact may be small or large, it may be in academic and not in social areas, it may have more impact on some areas of academic functioning than in others, and so on. Furthermore, it is taken for granted that factors other than LD may have a bearing on academic and social learning. Thus the initial goal of the assessment process is to make a determination of whether and to what extent LD impact on various academic and social learning/adaptation capacities.

To accomplish this purpose, it should go without saying that the neuropsychological assessment procedures should be reliable (Brown, Rourke, & Cicchetti, 1989) and valid (Rourke, 1991a). The principal dimensions of validity in the consideration of the clinical dimensions of assessment are those relating to content, concurrent, predictive, and ecological/clinical validity. The issues of content (or coverage) and concurrent validity are discussed just below; issues surrounding predictive validity are particularly relevant within the context of Steps 2 and 3; ecological/clinical validity is basic to all of the steps, but most specifically to considerations relevant to Steps 4 through 7.

Content validity—or, what we prefer to view as "coverage"—is a simple concept, but one with far-reaching ramifications. Simply put, a neuropsychological assessment has adequate content validity or coverage to the extent that it meets the following criteria: (a) the skill and

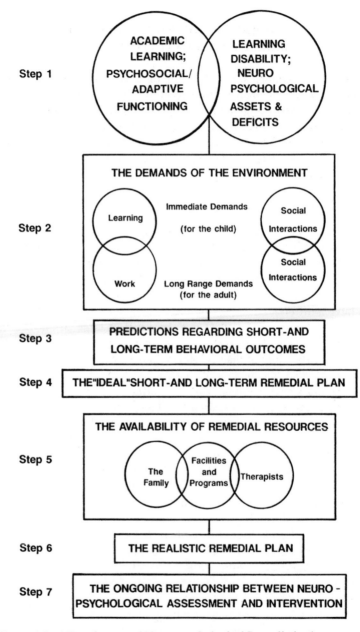

Figure 4.1. A Developmental Neuropsychological Remediation/Rehabilitation Model

ability domains tapped are sufficient to mirror the principal areas of functioning that are thought to be mediated by the brain, (b) the data gathered are sufficient to deal with the clinical (sometimes the referral) problems presented by the child. Failure to meet these criteria—that is, having poor content/coverage validity—can, and often does, severely limit our knowledge regarding the child's present neuropsychological status (concurrent validity), his or her probable prognosis with and without intervention (predictive validity), and the impact of the child's neuropsychological status on a reasonably broad spectrum of his or her developmental/adaptive task demands (ecological validity).

If one is interested merely in determining if a child has LD, the particular approach to assessment advocated by us is, for the most part, irrelevant. Adopting a more reasonable perspective—for example, one that invokes criteria of probable therapeutic relevance for determining the validity of a neuropsychological assessment—places the evaluation of coverage within a vastly different, and potentially more exciting, framework. Thus the evaluation of content/coverage validity within the context of ecological validity is tantamount to requiring that the content of the neuropsychological assessment (assuming for the moment that such content is adequately interpreted) must be fairly broad, pervasive, and comprehensive. It should be clear that such a goal will be achieved only through a reasonably painstaking analysis of a wide variety of functions, with attention being given to their interrelatedness and their dissociations.

To this end, we would propose that the ability and skill areas outlined in Table 4.1 constitute a bare minimum with respect to the dimensions that must be addressed in order to provide reasonable, relevant, and comprehensive answers to developmentally important clinical questions for children with LD. The reader should bear in mind that the specific tests and measures mentioned in Table 4.1 are of secondary importance. The crucial issues in the present context are matters related to the ability and skill domains that are sampled, and developmental considerations that bear upon levels of performance and complexity; the actual tests and measures employed must be evaluated against these issues and considerations. We should be quick to add that this categorization of skills and abilities lacks a firm scientific basis. However, the continuation of our work regarding the construct validity (dimensionality) of this test battery (Francis, Fletcher, & Rourke, 1988; Francis, Fletcher, Rourke, & York, 1992) is expected to yield such a basis.

TABLE 4.1   Tests Included in Neuropsychological Test Battery

Tactile-Perceptual

1. Reitan-Klove Tactile-Perceptual and Tactile-Forms Recognition Test
   a. Tactile Imperception and Suppression
   b. Finger Agnosia
   c. Fingertip Number-Writing Perception (9-15 yr)
      Fingertip Symbol-Writing Recognition (5-8 yr)
   d. Coin Recognition (9-15 yr)
      Tactile-Forms Recognition (5-8 yr)

Visual-Perceptual

1. Reitan-Klove Visual-Perceptual Tests
2. Target Test
3. Constructional Dyspraxia Items, Halstead-Wepman Aphasia Screening Test
4. WISC Picture Completion, Picture Arrangement, Block Design, Object Assembly subtests
5. Trail Making Test for Children, Part A (9-15 yr)
6. Color Form Test (5-8 yr)
7. Progressive Figures Test (5-8 yr)
   a. Matching Figures
   b. Star Drawing
   c. Matching Vs
   d. Concentric Squares Drawing

Auditory-Perceptual and Language Related

1. Reitan-Klove Auditory-Perceptual Test
2. Seashore Rhythm Test (9-15 yr)
3. Auditory Closure Test (Kass, 1964)
4. Auditory Analysis Test (Rosner & Simon, 1970)
5. Peabody Picture Vocabulary Test (Dunn, 1965)
6. Speech-Sounds Perception Test
7. Sentence Memory Test (Benton, 1965)
8. Verbal Fluency Test
9. WISC Information, Comprehension, Similarities, Vocabulary, Digit Span subtests
10. Aphasia Items, Aphasia Screening Test

TABLE 4.1 Continued

Problem Solving, Concept Formation, Reasoning

---

1. Halstead Category Test
2. Children's Word-Finding Test (Rourke & Fisk, 1976)
3. WISC Arithmetic subtest
4. Matching Pictures Test (5-8 yr)

Motor and Psychomotor

---

1. Reitan-Klove Lateral Dominance Examination
2. Dynamometer
3. Finger Tapping Test
4. Foot Tapping Test
5. Klove-Matthews Motor Steadiness Battery
   a. Maze Coordination Test
   b. Static Steadiness Test
   c. Grooved Pegboard Test

Other

---

1. Underlining Test (Doehring, 1968; Rourke & Gates, 1980; Rourke & Petrauskas, 1978)
2. WISC Coding subtest
3. Tactual Performance Test
4. Trail Making Test for Children, Part B (9-15 yr)

NOTE: Unless otherwise indicated, these measures are described in Reitan and Davison (1974) or Wechsler (1949, 1974). They are described extensively in Rourke (1989) and Rourke, Fisk, and Strang (1986).

Step 2: The Demands of the Environment

It is clear and evident that the results and dimensions of the neuro-psychological assessment described above—no matter how thorough and insightful—remain virtually useless until such time as they are related in a meaningful way to the developmental demands (behavioral tasks, skills, and abilities) that the child faces. This necessitates an appreciation on the part of the assessor of the sociohistorical-cultural milieu within which the child is expected to function. In North American society—

and, for the most part, that of Europe—the demands for learning in both academic and extra-academic milieux are quite well known. Some of these are immediate (short term, in the model); some, more far-flung (long term, in the model). Some have to do with formal learning environments such as the schoolroom; others, with informal learning situations such as play. All are important; hence all four sectors within the matrix associated with Step 2 need to be addressed. Failure to do so can, and often does, lead to terribly limited and even counterproductive forms of intervention for the child. (For examples of such outcomes see Rourke, Fisk, & Strang, 1986, especially chaps. 1, 5, and 6.)

Step 3: Predictions Regarding Short- and Long-Term Behavioral Outcomes

This step involves the formulation of prognoses for the individual child that flow from a melding of the conclusions arrived at in Steps 1 and 2: The child's neuropsychological assessment results are viewed within the context of the short- and long-term developmental demands that he or she is expected to face. In so doing, the relative ease or difficulty of these demands for the child can be seen within the context of the particular neuropsychological assets and deficits exhibited by him or her.

The formulation of confident prognostic statements is a complicated process that requires considerable experience with (a) those deficits in children at different ages that are expected to diminish or increase with the passage of time, with and without treatment, and (b) the relative impact of various forms of treatment on those deficits. The processes involved in the formulation of such prognostications are very much related to those required to deal with the next step in this model.

Step 4: The Ideal Short- and Long-Term Remedial Plans

Although seldom possible to put into practice, the formulation of ideal remedial plans offers an opportunity to "flesh out" the implications of Steps 1, 2, and 3. More important from a clinical perspective is the necessity to formulate a prognosis (or prognoses) that "fits" the neuropsychological status of the child. For example, it might be anticipated that a particular form of intervention (say, the institution of a synthetic phonics approach to single-word reading) would be beneficial in the short term, but counterproductive over the long haul. Such prognoses regarding the advisability of starting and stopping of appropriate treatments/interventions at particular times are often essential to the judgment of treatment efficacy. This approach to this phase of the assessment process also implies that the assessor will proffer some advice regarding the necessity for the type of assessment process that should be applied in order to determine whether a change of therapeutic/intervention tack would be advisable. Such an assessment could be as simple as the application of a standardized achievement test, to something as complex as a comprehensive examination (see Step 7).

Step 5: The Availability of Remedial Resources

The best therapeutic plans in the world cannot be applied without appropriate therapeutic resources. Hence it is necessary for the psychologist to be able to evaluate the therapeutic/intervention resources of the family, specialized "therapists," and the community. By *evaluation* we mean the fairly precise specification of the types of therapies and forms of intervention that the child with a specific subtype of LD needs and the likelihood that particular families, therapists, and other caregivers can and will provide them.

Perhaps the importance of this principle is best seen in an example of its breach: Very often, in our experience, the conclusions of standard psychoeducational assessments read like excerpts from the services offered by a particular school district. Suggestions like the following are common: placement in a LD class, phonics training, and referral to a speech pathologist. The results of any and, indeed, of all such recommendations may turn out to be quite productive. But it is far more common that such recommendations—lacking, as they do, much in specifications regarding precise modes of intervention, intensity, goals, and prognoses—form a very poor guide for the caregiver. What usually happens is that the therapists (teacher, speech pathologist, physiotherapist) must carry out their own assessments and relate their findings to what they view as their own therapeutic facilities. This is a very unproductive state of affairs, as it is wasteful of time, effort, and resources, and—of far more importance—causes unnecessary delays in the application of efficacious modes of intervention. Even worse, such shilly-shallying can lead to grossly inappropriate modes of intervention being applied.

Step 6: The Realistic Remedial Plan

The differences between Step 4 and Step 5 constitute the broad outline for the realistic remedial plan. When such differences are consistently large and/or consistently within one particular area (e.g., speech/language therapy) they constitute a "laundry list" of services required to address the needs of children with LD.

Step 7: The Ongoing Relationship Between
Neuropsychological Assessment and Intervention

In view of the changes that maturation and formal and informal learning experiences can effect, it is necessary to point out that neuropsychological and other forms of comprehensive assessment are not "one-shot" affairs. It should come as no surprise that repeated neuropsychological assessments are often required in order to fine-tune, or even grossly alter, remedial plans for children with LD.

Follow-up neuropsychological assessments also afford an opportunity to evaluate the effectiveness of particular modes of remedial intervention. Given our current (fairly abysmal) state of knowledge regarding the therapeutic efficacy of various forms of intervention for children with LD, a rigorous, objective, comprehensive, standardized assessment would appear to be a minimum requirement of any protocol designed to assess the effectiveness of these complex undertakings.

With these issues regarding assessment as background, we turn now to a consideration of issues relating to prognosis and treatment for the child who exhibits the NLD syndrome (subtype). We present these general principles as an example of the sort of treatment program that can emerge from the systematic, comprehensive analysis of children who exhibit a specific subtype of LD.

A TREATMENT PROGRAM FOR CHILDREN WITH NLD

The identification of subtypes of LD in combination with the intensive and comprehensive neuropsychological examination of the children with LD should provide insight into their disposition and treatment. One of the main objectives of subtyping efforts is to delineate with more precision the sorts of deficiencies that may account for a child's inability to acquire normal reading, spelling, or arithmetic skills so that these might be addressed in a treatment program. The comprehensive neuropsychological assessment further individualizes this process. The aim of this double-barreled process is to fashion remedial programs tailored to the individual's specific assets and deficits. Indeed it has been our clinical experience that a remedial management intervention that fails to "fit" the neurocognitive ability makeup of the child can, in effect, be counterproductive in respect to the acquisition of basic academic-related skills (Rourke, Fisk, & Strang, 1986).

Subtyping methods have an additional long-term economy in permitting the use of multivariate classification schemes that have some hope of being replicated in other clinical and research settings. In our experience such a systematic collection of data has proven to be helpful in the design, implementation, and validation of various treatment approaches. Some of the reasons for failure to replicate findings by independent investigators are either that there has not been sufficient denotation of the measurement operations or that the investigators have used different sets of performance measures. One can hardly expect to develop efficacious and generalizable treatment procedures when the assessment data have been collected by one-of-a-kind techniques.

The problem of translating neuropsychological assessment data into viable and effective educational and therapeutic procedures is not a simple one and has not yet been satisfactorily solved. Although a lack of experimental verification of treatment approaches is partly responsible for this state of affairs, there has also been the tendency for the educational community to favor the more traditional psychoeducational assessment for purposes of remedial planning. Unfortunately children who have been subjected to remedial regimens prescribed by this approach often make gains in skills that they practice, and yet exhibit little or no transfer-of-training to the classroom situation (Taylor, 1989).

As has been suggested in the past (Rourke, 1981), perhaps one of the main problems in bridging the gap between assessment information and intervention strategies lies in the lack of a sophisticated method for determining distinct groups of individual differences among children with LD that would allow for an adequate test of the presumed relationship between patterns of abilities and deficits and patterns of failure and success in the classroom. In the absence of any reliable and valid model of the child's cognitive ability structure, it is no wonder that most, if not all, academic remedial prescriptions can be viewed as speculative and having little hope of enjoying the luxury of a definitive empirical test. To complicate matters further, many educators seem to be more attached to the defense of professional turf rather than to the progress of scientific knowledge.

Still another factor of considerable importance in the treatment of children with LD involves the relationship between the child's ability-related assets and deficits and his or her adaptive capacities. There has been a tendency in the design of remedial programs to focus almost exclusively on the immediate demands of the academic milieu. Most often, scant attention is paid to the child's capacities to adapt to informal learning situations (e.g., play), social relationship requirements (within the family and with age-mates), and long-term learning and social developmental demands (Rourke, Fisk, & Strang, 1986). It is not enough simply to focus on promoting the child's academic growth while giving short shrift to issues of personal integration and psychosocial adjustment and adaptation.

Although there are a number of treatment programs for LD reported in the literature, very few have been demonstrated to be effective in well-controlled and replicated research (Taylor, 1989). An excellent summary of several of the factors critical in assessing the interaction between instructional methods and outcome for children with LD has been provided by Lyon and Flynn (1991). According to these investigators, the degree of relationship between learning-disability subtype, instructional treatment method, and outcome is difficult to interpret because of variations and/or limitations in variables such as the following: (a) measuring adherence to, or compliance with, a particular treatment strategy; (b) teacher-related variables, such as preparation or style; (c) specific classroom climate; and (d) the learning-disabled child's previous and concurrent instructional experiences. To complicate matters further, limited follow-up compliance, initial refusal to "experiment" with any given form of instruction, and delayed recognition of the effects of remediation pose additional problems when measuring the efficacy of remedial efforts. At the same time, the recent work of Fiedorowicz and Trites (1991) as well as Bakker (1986, 1990) and his associates (Bakker, Licht, & Van Strien, 1991) seems to hold promise in the effective treatment of subtypes of reading disorders in particular.

Our own work in this area has employed more in the way of clinical inferential rather than empirically based investigative strategies. For example, several single-case follow-up examinations of distinct subgroups of reading- and spelling-disordered children have shown them to be less amenable to instructional strategies that tend to be more "deficit-driven" rather than "compensatory" in nature. This appears to be the case in children who exhibit marked deficits in phonologic, symbolic, sequential, and/or mnemonic processing. In addition, neither age nor sex of the child appear to be contributing factors in differentiating outcome. Although the results of our research to date (Fuerst et al., 1989, 1990; Porter & Rourke, 1985; Rourke & Fuerst, 1991) would suggest that children whose LD seem due primarily to auditory-perceptual and/or psycholinguistic-related processing deficiencies tend to be generally well adjusted, those children who do experience some degree of emotional maladjustment seem to profit little from verbally biased psychotherapeutic techniques. This condition most likely reflects compromised verbal comprehension competencies, and may very well lead such children to avoid situations that are verbally interactive. Nevertheless the fact remains that the deficits that such children exhibit do not have a necessary negative impact on psychosocial functioning (Rourke & Fuerst, 1991).

As is the case of the psycholinguistically impaired youngster, most of the habilitational considerations for children with NLD are garnered from single-case follow-up investigations and reflect general principles of treatment intervention. We have attempted to relate the unique pattern of neuropsychological assets and deficits of such children to modes of intervention that are primarily, although not exclusively, compensatory in nature.

Our formulation of treatment strategies with children with NLD is based, in part, on a model of brain functioning that implicates the involvement of white matter disease or dysfunction in its manifestation (Rourke, 1989). This is of both theoretical and clinical importance in selecting the appropriate "mode" of intervention. For example, the earlier in development that white matter disease occurs, the more propitious it would be to utilize a treatment approach that attacks the deficits. This notion is predicated on the assumption that such an approach will serve to stimulate the functioning of the remaining white matter in order to foster the development of centers of gray matter. On the other hand, the longer the NLD syndrome persists, and the later its manifestation, the more likely that compensatory techniques will prove to be efficacious in pursuit of a therapeutic nature.

(For a complete explication of the specifics of this particular program, see the Appendix. The interested reader may also wish to access a recent presentation [Cermak & Murray, 1992] that describes in detail a treatment program for adults with NLD; this program is framed within the model of human occupation. Other approaches to treatment that have been derived clinically [Udwin & Yule, 1988, 1989] or subjected to some empirical validation [Williams et al., 1992] may also be of interest.)

Finally, it is clear that we need to establish whether and to what extent the specificity of subtype identification leads to specificity of efficacious treatments. Vapid debates regarding the relative utility of deficit- or compensatory-driven strategies at different stages of development will continue to be the rule until we make considerably more headway in this area. To this end, we need to focus on investigations in which preferred modes of intervention are deduced from models of neuropsychological relationships that have been shown to have concurrent and predictive validity. The work of Bakker and his associates (e.g., Bakker, 1986, 1990; Bakker et al., 1991) is one example of this approach; that of Lyon and associates (e.g., Lyon & Flynn, 1991) is another. Both of these approaches have shown considerable promise and we can expect to see more developments along these lines in the near future.

CONCLUSIONS AND GENERALIZATIONS

Neuropsychological assessment of children with LD and the interventive plans for such children that flow therefrom is a complex process that has several important dimensions. The sine qua non for the initiation of this process is a neuropsychological testing regimen and assessment procedure that is comprehensive, standardized, and amenable to a variety of methods of inference. This sets the stage for the application of the various "steps" involved in a comprehensive developmental model of neuropsychological remediation/habilitation. With respect to the latter, it is clear that each step in the process is inextricably interrelated, and that none should be viewed outside of the context of those that follow and/or precede it. Finally, it should be clear that there is very much to be done to validate commonly accepted and innovative forms of intervention for children with LD. Indeed, this is the most crying need in the field today.

5

A PROPOSED CLASSIFICATION OF LD SUBTYPES

As a final attempt to provide the reader with some structure regarding the subtyping efforts in the LD field and their implications for clinical practice, the following definitions and classification system are presented for perusal. No claim is made for the perspicacity of the formulations that follow: They are proffered as apparently reasonable generalizations that fit with our review of the reasonably well controlled studies that have appeared in the neuropsychological subtyping literature over the past 15 or so years.

A Note on Definitions. If there are reliable and valid differences between LD subtypes, and we still wish to retain the term *LD* as a generic descriptor of this heterogeneous group of disorders, then there are at least two issues with which we must deal.

1. There is a need for a generic definition. The current one(s) will probably do quite nicely. It might be well, however, to focus the generic definition on the common content of this group of disorders, namely, difficulties in learning in one or more areas.
2. There is a need for specific definitions of specific subtypes. Some of these (e.g., NLD) can be formulated now. Others will need to wait upon further research.

GENERIC DEFINITION

The following modification of the National Joint Committee on Learning Disabilities (January 30, 1981) definition would appear appropriate:

Learning disabilities is a generic term that refers to a heterogeneous group of disorders manifested by significant difficulties in the mastery of one or more of the following: listening, speaking, reading, writing, reasoning, mathematical, and other skills and abilities that are traditionally referred to as "academic." The term learning disabilities *is also appropriately applied in instances where persons exhibit significant difficulties in mastering social and other adaptive skills and abilities. In some cases, investigations of learning disabilities have yielded evidence that would be consistent with hypotheses relating central nervous system dysfunction to the disabilities in question. Even though a learning disability may occur concomitantly with other handicapping conditions (e.g., sensory impairment, mental retardation, social and emotional disturbance) or environmental influences (e.g., cultural differences, insufficient/inappropriate instruction, psychogenic factors), it is not the direct result of those conditions or influences. However, it is possible that emotional disturbances and other adaptive deficiencies may arise from the same patterns of central processing assets and deficits that generate the manifestations of academic and social learning disabilities.*

SPECIFIC DEFINITIONS (SUBTYPES)

All of the following subtypes are characterized in terms of the specific patterns of neuropsychological assets and deficits that are thought to be responsible for the particular patterns of learning assets and deficits exhibited by children within the subtype. Issues such as inadequate or inappropriate motivation or a mismatch between learning history and the specific demands of the academic environment are not dealt with. There are two dimensions emphasized, namely, the impact of the specific LD subtype (i.e., the specific pattern of neuropsychological assets and deficits) on (a) academic learning in the elementary school years and (b) socioemotional adaptation. With the exception of (B) below, these subtypal definitions have received very little investigative attention; they are more in the nature of hypotheses that could (and, we think, should) be investigated.

In proposing the patterns of neuropsychological assets and deficits that characterize these hypothesized LD subtypes, the reader should consult Figures 2.1, 2.2, and 2.3. The latter subtypes constitute rather well-defined entities and should serve as exemplars for the type of dynamic analysis that we feel should be determined for the other LD subtypes.

(A) Learning Disabilities Characterized Primarily by Disorders of Linguistic Functioning

(i) Basic Phonological Processing Disorder (BPPD)
Figure 2.3 contains a description of the dynamics of this subtype. As a summary of the assets and deficits that characterize this subtype, the following is offered.

Neuropsychological Assets:
Tactile perceptual, visual-spatial-organizational, psychomotor, and nonverbal problem-solving and concept-formation skills and abilities are developed to an average to above-average degree. The capacity to deal with novelty and the amount and quality of exploratory behavior are average. Attention to tactile and visual input is normal.

Neuropsychological Deficits:
Disordered phonemic hearing, segmenting, and blending are paramount. Attention to and memory for auditory-verbal material are clearly impaired. Poor verbal reception, repetition, and storage are evident. Amount and quality of verbal associations are clearly underdeveloped. There is a less than average amount of verbal output.

Prognoses:

Academic. Reading and spelling are affected as are those aspects of arithmetic performance that require reading and writing. The symbolic aspects of writing are affected. The nonverbal aspects of arithmetic and mathematics are left unaffected. The prognosis for advances in reading and spelling and the verbal-symbolic aspects of writing and arithmetic must be very guarded.

Psychosocial. Psychosocial disturbance may occur if parents, teachers, and other caretakers establish unattainable goals for the child and/or if antisocial models and lifestyles hold reinforcing properties for the child that the school is unable to provide. When psychopathology occurs, it is likely to be of the acting-out variety. Another possibility is mild anxiety/depression.

(ii) Phoneme-Grapheme Matching Disorder (PGMD)
With reference to Figure 2.3 and the description of the BPPD subtype, the following assets, deficits, and prognoses appear to apply.

Neuropsychological Assets:
Identical to the BPPD subtype, except that phonemic hearing, segmenting, and blending are normal.

Neuropsychological Deficits:
Phoneme-grapheme (most often: grapheme → phoneme) matching problems are paramount.

Prognoses:

Academic. Written spelling of words known "by sight" may be average or better; written spelling of words not known "by sight" is as poor as in the BPPD subtype. Word-recognition is much better than that exhibited by the BPPD subtype, although still at an impaired level. Word-decoding skills may be as poor as for the BPPD subtype. Arithmetic and mathematics performances may rise to average or above-average levels when the words involved in performance on problems in this domain are minimized or learned by sight. The prognosis for advances in reading and spelling is fair and much better than that for the BPPD subtype. Prognoses for advancement in arithmetic and mathematics are good under the conditions mentioned above. Writing of unfamiliar words continues to be problematic.

Psychosocial. The prognosis for socioemotional disturbance is the same as that for the BPPD subtype, but with somewhat less risk.

(iii) Word-Finding Disorder (WFD)
This subtype is characterized by outstanding problems in word-finding and verbal expressive skills within a context of a wide range of intact neuropsychological skills and abilities.

Neuropsychological Assets:
Identical to those of the PGMD subtype, except that phoneme-grapheme matching skills are intact.

Neuropsychological Deficits:
The only outstanding deficit is difficulty in accessing a normal store of verbal associations.

Prognoses:

Academic. Reading and spelling are very poor during early school years, with near-average or average performances in these areas emerging toward the end of the elementary school period (i.e., at approximately Grades 6 to 8). Arithmetic and mathematics are seen as early strengths. Writing of words that can be expressed and writing from a model are average to good.

Psychosocial. Prognosis for socioemotional functioning is virtually normal, but with the added minor risk factor of early failure in school.

(B) Learning Disabilities Characterized Primarily by Disorders of Nonverbal Functioning

The NLD Syndrome (see Figure 2.1 and 2.2)

Neuropsychological Assets:
Auditory-verbal perception, attention, and memory become well developed. Simple motor tasks and those that can be learned by rote are well accomplished. Good phonological skills are seen fairly early in development. Verbal reception, repetition, storage, and associations are evident from the early school years onward. A high volume of verbal output characterizes this subtype.

Neuropsychological Deficits:
Tactile and visual perception deficits are evident early in development; these include attention to and memory for material delivered through these modalities. Complex psychomotor tasks, except those that can be learned through extensive repetition, are poorly performed. An aversion to novel experiences, with consequent negative impact on exploratory behavior, characterizes this subtype. Problems in age-appropriate concept formation and problem solving are especially evident. The principal deficits in linguistic skills are those relating to the content and pragmatic dimensions of language. In addition, language is often used for inappropriate purposes.

Prognoses:

Academic. Word-decoding and spelling often develop to superior levels. Verbatim memory, especially for material of an auditory-verbal nature, becomes very well developed. Areas of emerging and continuing concern include reading comprehension, mechanical arithmetic, mathematics, and science. Some dimensions of "science" and "mathematics" can be learned if the material is presented and practiced in a rote fashion; difficulties become apparent when reasoning, deduction, and the like are required.

Psychosocial. Basic problems in perception, judgment, problem solving, and reasoning lead to difficulties in social competence. Risk for moderate to severe psychopathology, especially of the internalized variety, is high. Activity level tends to decline to hypoactive levels by late childhood. Long-term prognosis for socioemotional development is very guarded.

(C) Learning Disabilities Characterized Primarily by Output Disorders in All Modalities

This subtype is similar to the WFD subtype with respect to neuropsychological assets and deficits. Within the academic realm, there are the added problems of deficient output in the writing of words and written arithmetic.

Neuropsychological Assets:
Identical to WFD subtype.

Neuropsychological Deficits:
Identical to WFD subtype, with the additional difficulty of organizing, directing, and orchestrating all aspects of behavioral expression.

Prognoses:

Academic. Rather severe problems in oral and written output are prominent in early school years. Marked advances in word-recognition, word-decoding, and reading comprehension are evident in the middle school years. Written work remains poor, as does the capacity to deliver verbal descriptions and answers to questions.

Psychosocial. Such children are often characterized as having "acting-out" disorders in early school years. They are also at risk for social withdrawal and depression. This may develop into full-blown externalized and/or internalized forms of psychopathology if management by the child's principal caretakers is inappropriate.

We turn now to a discussion of case studies that exemplify the dynamics of three of the above-mentioned sybtypes.

6

CASE STUDIES

The case studies presented in this chapter are an illustration of the application of the neuropsychological approach to the assessment of childhood learning disabilities that we have outlined in the previous chapters. We have chosen these case studies in order to point out various subtypes of LD assessed in terms of neuropsychological principles, as well as modes of intervention that are deduced from models of neuropsychological relationships.

The three case reports that follow are, in effect, a culmination of the developmental neuropsychological approach to the study of LD presented throughout this book. To iterate, it is an approach that seeks to understand problems in learning by studying developmental changes in behavior as seen through the perspective of brain-behavior models. It is, in essence, an approach that combines the study of development of the brain with the study of the development of behavior. Specifically, with respect to the child with LD, the aspects of this approach that are most relevant are those that have to do with proposed linkages between patterns of central processing assets and deficits that may predispose a youngster to predictably different patterns of learning failure.

To facilitate discussion, each of the three case presentations has been assigned a gender-appropriate pseudonym. The general format for the presentations involves an introduction containing some information regarding the patient, a presentation of the neuropsychological test results, and a discussion of the findings. The test results are arranged in a manner that is meant to facilitate their interpretation within the context of the developmental neuropsychological approach that has been articulated in the previous chapters. The tests employed in this battery are described in Table 4.1 and are discussed at some length in Rourke et al. (1983) and Rourke, Fisk, and Strang (1986). Some notes regarding the format of data presentation are in order, as follows.

1. In these case descriptions, the terms *severe, moderate, mild, borderline, average,* and *superior* are used to describe levels of impairment on tests within the various areas discussed. On the basis of the Knights and Norwood (1980) and other norms for these tests, these terms indicate the following levels of impairment:

   A. *Severe* means more than 3 standard deviations below the mean for the age of the child;
   B. *Moderate* means between 2 and 3 standard deviations below the mean;
   C. *Mild* means between 1 and 2 standard deviations below the mean;
   D. *Borderline* means close to 1 standard deviation below the mean;
   E. *Average* means between 1 standard deviation below and 1 standard deviation above the mean; and
   F. *Superior* means performance that exceeds 1 standard deviation above the mean.

2. A range of *T* scores from 10 to 70 is used throughout. Those scores that fall below 10 and above 70 are assigned scores of 10 and 70, respectively. This poses a significant problem only for scores that are considerably higher than 70; these are pointed out in the textual account of the assessment.

3. To facilitate interpretation, the WISC-R and WRAT-R summary measures are presented in numerical format. In addition, a discussion of the results of parent- and teacher-completed behavior questionnaires can be found in the text of each case.

4. Because of the nature of the qualitative analysis of responses on the Aphasia Screening Test, test results are also presented in textual, rather than graphical, form.

CASE I: MICHAEL (BASIC PHONOLOGICAL PROCESSING DISORDER)

This case is presented in order to illustrate the neuropsychological study of a child with a linguistic, verbally based learning disability. This case is an example of the BPPD (Group R-S) subtype described in previous chapters.

Relevant History

This youngster was referred for neuropsychological assessment by his family physician for evaluation of chronic learning and behavioral problems. At the time of this assessment, Michael was 10 years of age and was the recipient of special education assistance in the areas of reading, spelling, and language arts. This assistance had been provided to him since Grade 1. In addition to his learning difficulties, his mother indicated that Michael had been recently exhibiting behavioral problems characterized by poor temper and anger control, aggressivity, oppositionality, and poor responsiveness to disciplinary actions. She described Michael as exhibiting problems in concentration and attentional deployment, distractibility, motoric disinhibition, and modulation of mood.

A review of this youngster's past developmental history revealed that he was the product of a full-term, normal cephalic delivery. Birth weight was 8 lb, 5 oz. There were no significant gestational complications reported, and his immediate postnatal growth and development proceeded fairly normally. Although motor milestones were achieved at age expectancy levels, early sentence structure difficulties were noted. His past medical history was noteworthy for frequent early ear infections, a tonsillectomy, and an adenoidectomy at age 5, a broken wrist at age 7, and broken teeth at 2 and 5 years of age secondary to accidental falls. Episodes of loss of consciousness were denied. He had no known history of allergies and he was not currently on any prescribed medications. To the best of our knowledge, no other psychological, psychiatric, or neuropsychological consultations had been conducted on this youngster.

He presented with a rather complicated psychosocial history. His biological parents divorced in 1972, when Michael was approximately 2 years of age. His biological father was a carnival worker who had completed 8 years of formal education. Visitation with this gentleman was infrequent and occurred approximately twice yearly. Michael's biological mother was employed as a medical assistant and had completed 14 years of formal education. She remarried approximately 5 years prior to this assessment to a gentleman who was employed as a tool maker. He had completed 11 years of formal education. By the mother's report, this gentleman was an alcoholic. Though the mother admitted to a history of verbal and physical abuse of her by her current husband, she denied any such behavior levied against Michael.

The family members included a 14-year-old biological sister, as well as two half-sisters ($2\frac{1}{2}$ and 4 years of age). There was a history reminiscent of LD in Michael's biological sister. There was also a history of LD in the biological father as well as a maternal uncle. At the time of this assessment, all six family members resided in a mobile home where space limitations reportedly caused some stress among family members.

Academically, Michael was enrolled in a split one-half regular Grade 3/one-half special education classroom setting. Teacher reports described Michael's academic performance as being far below grade level in the areas of reading and writing, somewhat below grade level in the areas of arithmetic and spelling, and at grade level in the areas of social studies and science.

Behavioral Observations During the Examination

Although this youngster was generally well behaved during the actual assessment sessions, he was initially shy and withdrawn. Rapport with the examiner improved as the testing progressed, although Michael did seem to require a fair amount of support and reassurance regarding his performance. He was mildly fidgety and restless but not necessarily motorically driven. Attentional capacities were generally adequate and there was no evidence of any marked distractibility. Perhaps the most prominent features of his test-taking behavior were his tendency to proceed with tasks before instructions were completed and his somewhat poor self-monitoring habits. Frustration tolerance also appeared to be somewhat limited as he exhibited a tendency to give up rather easily on seemingly more difficult tasks. Mild problems in his understanding of test instructions were also noted, necessitating frequent repetition of task directives. All things considered, it was felt that the current test results represented a fairly reliable and valid reflection of his neurocognitive and behavioral functioning.

Test Results and Interpretations

Michael's test results are summarized in Figure 6.1 and Table 6.1. Lateral dominance examination suggested this youngster to be exclusively right-handed, right-footed, and right-eyed. Psychomotor examination revealed average performances bilaterally on measures of upper extremity motoric strength, kinetic and static motor steadiness, and speeded fine eye-hand coordination. He also exhibited an average level of performance with his right hand on a measure of finger oscillation speed, whereas left-handed performance on this task was mildly slowed.

There was no compelling evidence of any tactile imperception or suppression. Although he exhibited low-average performances bilaterally on haptic perceptual measures involving finger dysgraphesthesia and astereognosis, finger agnosia testing yielded a markedly impaired

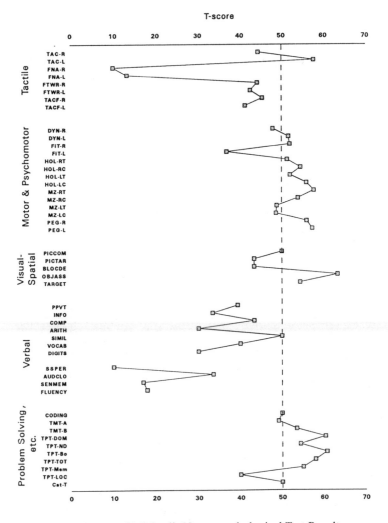

Figure 6.1. Summary of Michael's Neuropsychological Test Results

NOTE: Explanations of abbreviations: *Tactile:* TAC-R, tactile-perceptual abilities, right hand; TAC-L, tactile-perceptual abilities, left hand; FNA-R, finger agnosia, right hand; FNA-L, finger agnosia, left hand; FTWR-R, fingertip number-writing, right hand; FTWR-L, fingertip number-writing, left hand; TACF-R, tactile-forms recognition, right hand; TACF-L, tactile-forms recognition, left hand.

Motor & Psychomotor: DYN-R, dynamometer (strength of grip), right hand; DYN-L, dynamometer (strength of grip), left hand; FiT-R, finger tapping, right hand; FiT-L, finger tapping, left hand; HOT-RT, Graduated Holes Test, time, right hand; HOL-RC, Graduated Holes Test, contact, right hand; HOL-LT, Graduated Holes Test, time, left hand; HOL-LC, Graduated Holes Test, contact, left hand;

performance with each hand. Performance on a complex tactually guided problem-solving task (involving tactile form discrimination, manual dexterity, and haptic kinesthetic feedback) was above average with his right hand and average with his left hand. A third, conjoint hand trial yielded an above-average level of performance. A measure of incidental learning performance on this task yielded an average score, while his performance was mildly impaired on a measure of topographical memory.

There was no indication of any visual imperception or suppression, although he had some difficulty fixating his gaze during visual field testing. A measure of visual acuity yielded 20/20 performances bilaterally. His drawings of simple geometric configurations were reasonably well executed while his rendition of a complex key was somewhat primitive and lacking in fine detail. Name writing performance with the right hand was mildly slowed, whereas that with the left hand was average. Qualitatively, his name writing performance suggested that he was still in the process of consolidating his cursive writing skills. There was no compelling evidence of any dysgraphia in any of his printed script performances.

An associative learning task involving speed and accuracy of symbolic transcription was performed in an average fashion, and he had no difficulty remembering or reproducing graphically sequences of visual stimuli. Speed of performance was average on a visual-spatial negotiation task performed under either simple (involving numerical cues only) or more complex (involving symbolic shifting between alphabetic and numeric sequences) conditions. Several seemingly impulsive errors were noted on this task, however.

MZ-RT, Maze Test, time, right hand; MZ-RC, Maze Test, contact, right hand; MZ-LT, Maze Test, time, left hand; MZ-LC, Maze Test, contact, left hand; PEG-R, Grooved Pegboard, right hand; PEG-L Grooved Pegboard, left hand.

Visual-Spatial: PICCOM, WISC-R Picture Completion; PICTAR, WISC-R Picture Arrangement; BLOCDE, WISC-R Block Design; OBJASS, WISC-R Object Assembly; TARGET, Target Test.

Verbal: PPVT, Peabody Picture Vocabulary Test; INFO, WISC-R Information; COMP, WISC-R Comprehension; ARITH, WISC-R Arithmetic; SIMIL, WISC-R Similarities; VOCAB, WISC-R Vocabulary; DIGITS, WISC-R Digit Span; SSPER, Speech-Sounds Perception Test; AUDCLO, Auditory Closure Test; SENMEM, Sentence Memory Test; FLUENCY, Verbal Fluency Test.

Problem Solving, Etc.: CODING, WISC-R Coding; TMT-A, Trail Making Test, Part A; TMT-B, Trail Making Test, Part B; TPT-Dom, Tactual Performance Test, dominant hand; TPT-ND, Tactual Performance Test, nondominant hand; TPT-Bo, Tactual Performance Test, both hands; TPT-TOT, Tactual Performance Test, total; TPT-Mem, Tactual Performance Test, memory; TOT-LOC, Tactual Performance Test, location; Cat-T, Category Test.

TABLE 6.1   Summary of Michael's Test Results at 10 Years, 0 Months

	Testing at 10 yrs, 0 mo
WISC-R	
VIQ	80
PIQ	100
FSIQ	91
Underlining (no. of each)	
Superior	1
Average	4
Borderline	0
Mild	3
Moderate	4
Severe	2
Speed Subtest	Average
WRAT-R (grade/centile)	
Reading	1/.06
Spelling	1/.4
Arithmetic	3/6
PIC-R (T score)	
Lie	42
F	53
Defensiveness	30
Adjustment	85
Achievement	71
Intellectual Screening	91
Development	59
Somatic Concern	50
Depression	67
Family Relations	69
Delinquency	99
Withdrawal	47
Anxiety	63
Psychosis	52
Hyperactivity	46
Social Skills	62

He exhibited average performances on the initial 3 subtests of the Underlining Test (a series of 14 subtests involving the rapid underlining of various verbal and nonverbal stimuli interspersed among various distractor items), which was then followed by an above-average level of performance on the 4th subtest. On the subsequent 9 subtests his performance clustered around the moderately to markedly impaired range. These latter subtests involved the detection of more verbally and/or sequentially complex stimuli.

A Performance IQ of 100 was in evidence on the WISC-R. Subtest performances within this section of the WISC-R ranged from low-average on tasks designed to assess his ability to comprehend a story as told in pictures and to construct abstract visual-spatial designs out of colored blocks (Picture Arrangement and Block Design subtest scaled scores of 8) to an above-average performance on a "puzzle-like" assembly task (Object Assembly subtest scaled score of 14). He exhibited average performances on tasks involving the identification of the missing parts in pictures of commonly encountered objects and the associating of symbols to their appropriate numerical counterparts (Picture Completion and Coding subtest scaled scores of 10).

There was no evidence of any auditory imperception or suppression, and his performance was within normal limits on a Pure Tone Sweep Hearing Test. Although he exhibited mildly impaired performances on sound-blending and nonverbal rhythmic discrimination tasks, his performances clustered around the markedly impaired range on phoneme-grapheme matching, phonemically cued verbal fluency, and phonemic discrimination/segmentation measures.

He was only able to recall immediately four digits forward and two digits backward (a moderately impaired level of performance), and he encountered a good deal of difficulty on a task involving the immediate recall for sentences of gradually increasing length. On the other hand, he exhibited low average immediate recall and long-term storage scores in the context of average long-term retrieval and consistent long-term retrieval performances on the Buschke Selective Reminding Test, a task requiring memory for a series of unrelated words (Buschke, 1974).

His performance was replete with errors on a brief screening test designed to measure the symbolic and communicational aspects of language. For example, he spelled the word *square* as *sa,* the word *cross* as *kach,* and the word *triangle* as *anlk.* When asked to name a picture of a clock, he initially responded "wa, no, clock." When asked to print the name of this object, he began by writing *Kl* (presumably for the word *clock)*, *W* (presumably for the word *watch)*, and then the letter *K.* When asked to write down the phrase *he shouted the warning,* he wrote *he shta a the waing.* He read the phrase *7 six 2* as *772, 72,* the phrase *SEE THE BLACK DOG* as *see the boy poke,* and the phrase *PLACE LEFT HAND TO RIGHT EAR* as *place went wrench to which where.* Several other reading errors were noted as well. He also encountered problems repeating verbatim some complex multisyllabic words. He solved the written computation 85 − 27 as 52, and arrived at the answer 15 for the written computation 55 − 29. In response to the command, "place left hand to right ear," he initially placed his right hand to his right ear and then self-corrected his response. Performance on the PPVT-R yielded a standard score of 84, a centile ranking of 14, and an age equivalency of 8-1 years.

This youngster exhibited a Verbal IQ of 80 on the WISC-R. Subtest performances within this portion of the WISC-R ranged from moderately impaired on tasks designed to assess his fund of factual knowledge and his "mental" numerical reasoning capacities (Information and Arithmetic subtest scaled scores of 5 and 4, respectively) to an average performance on a verbal reasoning task involving the ability to identify the underlying conceptual link between various word pairs (Similarities subtest scaled score of 10). His performance clustered around the low average range on tasks designed to assess his understanding of appropriate social mores and customs and the integrity of his verbal lexicon (Comprehension and Vocabulary subtest scaled scores of 8 and 7, respectively).

Although he encountered no difficulty on a problem-solving task involving some degree of nonverbal concept formation, hypothesis testing, and the ability to benefit from positive and negative informational feedback, his performance was markedly impaired on a measure of verbal deductive reasoning.

Brief academic achievement testing with the WRAT-R (Jastak & Wilkinson, 1984) yielded the following standard score equivalents: Reading (word-recognition), 49; Spelling, 56; Arithmetic, 77. Based on this youngster's chronological age, these scores correspond to centile rankings (grade equivalents) of .06 (1M), .4 (1M), and 6 (3B), respectively. His written misspellings revealed several phonemic omissions, while he tended to utilize a "best guess" strategy based on the most salient phonemic cues in his reading of novel, unfamiliar words. For example, in response to the word *finger* he responded "fi ing ger" and then responded "her." At times, it also appeared as though he utilized a "best guess" strategy based on the most salient visual characteristics of the words to be read.

To obtain some information regarding this youngster's socioemotional and behavioral adjustment, the mother was asked to complete the Personality Inventory for Children-Revised. In addition, school personnel completed the Connors Teacher Rating Scale (Goyette, Connors, & Ulrich, 1978) and the Achenbach Child Behavior Checklist (Edelbrock & Achenbach, 1984). From a parental perspective, this youngster was described as exhibiting rather significant behavioral problems in the areas of self-control and self-discipline. Features of oppositionality (subsuming characteristics of quarrelsomeness, disobedience, and defiance), impulsivity, emotional lability, heightened motoric activity, distractibility and inattentiveness, limited frustration tolerance, and poor anger control were acknowledged by primary caretakers. In the aggregate, this youngster's behavior appears to be much less problematic within the school environment, with teacher reports tending to emphasize his distractibility and inattentiveness tendencies. Much of this appears to be present during the execution of highly academically biased tasks (e.g., reading and spelling).

Summary, Impressions, and Recommendations

In the aggregate, this youngster's psychometric protocol revealed a constellation of neurocognitive performance inefficiencies that were consistent with a language and/or verbally based learning disability (of the Basic Phonological Processing variety). These included a rather underdeveloped appreciation for the phonological and/or acoustical structure of language, mild auditory verbal mnestic difficulties, deficient verbal mediation competencies, and mild serial order and/or sequencing problems. It was likely that these particular deficiencies were the primary factors responsible for his poorly developed word recognition and written spelling competencies. His poorly developed auditory analysis skills were clearly evident in his actual attempts at encoding and decoding novel, unfamiliar words. Formal standardized testing of achievement levels revealed performances in these areas that were consistent with the average child in a beginning Grade 1 program.

It is important to note that this youngster performed reasonably well on a number of tasks designed to assess the integrity of his visual perceptual, perceptual organizational, and visual-constructive capacities. Visual analytic reasoning abilities appeared to be adequately developed, including his ability to abstract and develop concepts with visually presented (largely nonverbal) information. In general, nonverbal problem-solving abilities (including tactually guided problem-solving competency) appeared to be significantly better developed than were verbal conceptual reasoning skills. There was also no evidence of any significant deficiencies on tasks designed to assess his simple and more complex psychomotor competencies.

In terms of socioemotional and behavioral adjustment difficulties, this youngster was described by primary caretakers as exhibiting a number of behavioral features commonly associated with an oppositional defiant disturbance. These included elements of quarrelsomeness, disobedience, difficulty adhering to adult-imposed rules, and poor anger and impulse control. School personnel tended to highlight mild problems with concentration and attentional deployment, but otherwise his behavior was largely unremarkable within the classroom environment.

In terms of treatment intervention, it was suggested that this youngster would probably benefit substantially from academic remedial strategies that tend to be more compensatory rather than deficit-driven in nature. That is to say, remediation techniques should be directed toward capitalizing upon this youngster's better developed visual-perceptual and nonverbal problem-solving skills. For example, this youngster would probably benefit from programs that tend to place a greater focus upon visual or "whole word" approaches to instruction in reading and spelling. The "word family," "chunking," or any such program that tends to emphasize the structural, as opposed to phonetic, units of words would be appropriate in this regard. The Morphographic Spelling Program (Dixon & Engelman, 1979) is an example of such an approach.

Although remediation should not necessarily eschew attempts at developing further this youngster's auditory analysis skills, a developmental neuropsychological model would predict that children who fail to display significant progress in the development of their phonological abilities by the age of 9 or 10 years are not likely to do so to any substantial extent thereafter. Should any remediation of his auditory analysis skills continue, however, it was suggested that the initial stages of such training utilize words that are familiar to him. More complex, novel words could then be introduced as his ability to engage in the auditory analysis of graphic language improves. Other remediation techniques that were suggested included the development of his serial order and/or sequencing skills, as well as development of his verbal remediation abilities. Self-repetition and paraphrasing of auditorially presented instructions may be helpful in this connection.

To address this youngster's behavioral adjustment problems, it was suggested that the parents enroll in some type of behavioral management program. His mild attentional problems at school appeared to be largely task-specific, occurring predominantly during spelling endeavors. In the context of this youngster's neurocognitive ability deficits, this was, of course, not particularly surprising. Nevertheless, it was recommended that improvement of his attentional capacities be addressed through some type of school-based behavioral modification program. The school psychologist was thought to be in a particularly good position to serve as an important consultant in this regard.

Discussion

Although school personnel had already identified and certified this youngster as learning disabled prior to this consultation, the specific ability deficits contributing to his learning problems had not been clearly delineated. Previous psychoeducational examinations of this youngster merely "diagnosed" his condition based on an evaluation of intelligence and achievement status and a limited sampling of his socioemotional and behavioral functioning. Emphasizing more of a diagnostic rather than a descriptive approach, these examinations, in actuality, provided little if any clinically useful information from which to develop viable and effective educational and therapeutic procedures.

Comprehensive neuropsychological examination of this youngster provided insight into his disposition and treatment. The examination procedures helped to delineate with more precision the sorts of deficiencies that may account for his inability to acquire normal reading, spelling, and arithmetic skills so that these might be addressed in a treatment program. The comprehensive neuropsychological assessment further identified this youngster's neurocognitive assets and strengths. The aim of this double-barreled process was to fashion a remedial program that was more tailored to this youngster's specific assets and deficits.

The problem of translating neuropsychological assessment data into viable and effective educational and therapeutic procedures is usually not a simple one and frequently cannot be satisfactorily solved. Although a lack of experimental verification of treatment approaches is partly responsible for this state of affairs, it is also the case that the educational community tends to favor the more traditional psychoeducational assessment for purposes of remedial planning. Nonetheless an educational conference was arranged with school personnel for purposes of discussing the presumed relationship between this youngster's patterns of neurocognitive ability deficits and patterns of failure and success in the classroom. While his current remedial program was largely "deficit driven" (without knowing the specific ability deficits) in nature, it was suggested to school personnel that the focus of treatment should be to exploit this youngster's neurocognitive strengths for compensatory modes of adaptation.

In general the older and more impaired the child, the more likely it is that compensatory techniques accentuating the use of the child's assets will be found to be effective and should dominate the treatment picture. The emphasis that we have brought to the understanding of this youngster's learning problems is one that attempts to integrate dimensions of individual development on the one hand with relevant central information processing (i.e., neurocognitive) features on the other—all of this in order to fashion a useful approach with which to remediate his academic difficulties.

Clinical interview and behavioral data also highlighted the presence of a number of troublesome and disruptive behavioral tendencies in this youngster. Because much of this appeared to be manifested within the home environment, management of his behavioral problems was addressed in the context of a structured parenting program. The intent of this intervention was to provide parents with the ability to define, assess, and remediate the problem behaviors of this youngster. The program was successful if for no other reason than introducing primary caretakers to a method of behavioral analysis and change. Follow-up discussion with the parents one year later suggested that the program continued to provide a therapeutic framework for the management of this youngster's behavior, despite the necessity of episodic parent "retraining" sessions throughout this period.

School personnel were also provided with an extensive, but by no means exhaustive, collection of suggestions for behaviorally altering this youngster's mild attentional difficulties. Where possible, it was advised that the school psychologist be consulted for additional information and support in implementation of these suggestions.

CASE 2: DAVID (NONVERBAL LEARNING DISABILITIES)

This case is presented in order to illustrate the clinical manifestations of the Nonverbal Learning Disability (NLD) syndrome. Children in this group are normally found to exhibit outstanding problems in visual-spatial-organizational, tactile-perceptual, psychomotor, and nonverbal problem-solving skills, within a context of clear strengths in psycholinguistic skills, such as rote verbal learning, phoneme-grapheme matching, verbal output, and verbal classification. Academically, such children are seen to experience major learning difficulties in mechanical arithmetic, while exhibiting advanced levels of word-recognition and spelling. From a socioemotional perspective, it is common to find that children with NLD have interactional problems with their peers, as well as being prone to withdraw from novel social situations (Rourke, 1982, 1987, 1989; Rourke & Strang, 1978, 1983). It has been hypothesized that their somewhat deficient (nonverbal) logical reasoning abilities (particularly under novel conditions) are a major factor contributing to this situation. New situations seem to pose a serious problem for them because of the large number of cues that must be interpreted properly in order to understand fully the social interactions that are proceeding and the specific requirements demanded from or for each individual in them. Another factor that seems to contribute to their social inadequacies is their difficulty in attending to and/or providing nonverbal cues. Facial expressions, hand movements, body postures, and other physical gestures are forms of nonverbal communication that are important for success in novel social situations. The perception and understanding of these forms of communication seem to be deficient in youngsters with NLD.

The main points of the following description deal with the findings of an initial assessment conducted on David at 11 years of age. This is followed by a brief summary of the major findings of a second assessment conducted on this youngster when he was 12 years, 11 months of age. It should be noted that there was little change in David's pattern of neuropsychological test results from the first to the second assessment; however, there were some changes evident in his level of performance on several tasks.

Relevant History

This 11-year-old Caucasian youngster was referred for neuropsychological assessment after a significant verbal-performance difference was found on recent psychometric intelligence testing. A specific question had been raised as to whether this boy may be suffering from some type of central processing disturbance. Associated concerns included poorly developed reading comprehension capacities, as well as problems of social isolation.

Developmentally, this youngster was born at term with a breech presentation. Birth weight was 7 lb. 14 oz. There were no significant gestational complications reported, and his early developmental history was characterized as unremarkable. Both motor and language milestones were achieved at age-expectancy levels. Past medical history was unremarkable. No major injuries or childhood illnesses were reported. Two years prior to this assessment this youngster underwent school conducted psychometrics for evaluation of emotional, adjustment, and/or behavioral problems. He was referred for psychiatric evaluation at that time and was seen by a psychiatrist for two sessions. He had not previously received any type of neurological examination or neuropsychological assessment.

Psychosocial history revealed this youngster to be the youngest in a biological sibship of three. Two of David's older brothers completed advanced levels of education, while a 16-year-old brother was performing satisfactorily in high school. David's biological mother graduated from college and was an accountant by trade, and his biological father was a professional within the health care field. Significant developmental, medical, and psychological/psychiatric problems were denied among immediate family members.

Behavioral Observations During the Examination

This youngster was quite cooperative and seemingly well motivated throughout the testing proceedings. Nonetheless, he displayed little enthusiasm or interest in the tasks, and he made little attempt to establish a cordial or friendly relationship with the examiner. David did not, for example, spontaneously volunteer additional information, and he tended to respond to the examiner's questions regarding his interest, friends, and favored activities in a terse, business-like manner. He averted eye contact throughout the session, and he displayed a limited range of positive or negative emotions. Smiling was seldom noticed and he could perhaps best be described as being somewhat emotionally "constricted." Despite a rather perfunctory attitude toward the testing, he persisted in difficult tasks without prompts or encouragement. Although he displayed little frustration or anxiety while completing challenging tasks (such as a test of problem solving and concept formation), he agreed that these tests were difficult. All things considered, it was felt that the test results obtained appeared to constitute a fairly reliable and valid measure of David's neurocognitive and adaptive capacities.

Test Results and Interpretations

David's test results are summarized in Figure 6.2 and Table 6.2. A lateral preference examination revealed this youngster to be exclusively right-handed, right-footed, and right-eyed. Tests of simple motor speed with both the upper and lower extremities yielded moderately slowed performances bilaterally, with performance being relatively slower on the right side of his body. Strength of grip, however, was within normal limits bilaterally. Tests for kinetic motor steadiness were performed in an above-average manner with each hand, while motor steadiness testing within the static disposition revealed mild tremulousness bilaterally. David's performance on a speeded fine eye-hand coordination task was significantly impaired with each hand. Difficulties he encountered on this task were felt, in part, to reflect visual-spatial deficits in orienting the pegs to the board. This interpretation was consistent with David's difficulties in drawing a key and copying geometric forms. Although David included adequate detail in his drawings, he made consistent errors in estimating their size and in "integrating" the various parts of the drawings to form a cohesive gestalt.

David's performance on a tactual perceptual exam revealed consistent evidence of bilateral deficits. Although no evidence of simple tactile imperceptions or suppressions were observed, his performance on tests of finger agnosia and dysgraphesthesia was markedly impaired bilaterally. Performance on a simple test of tactile recognition of geometric forms, however, was average.

His performance on a more complex test of tactile and kinesthetic perceptual abilities was markedly impaired. David's first trial with his right hand on this test of nonverbal problem solving (involving tactile form recognition and tactually guided behavior) was markedly impaired. His responses on this trial indicated that he was employing an inefficient problem-solving strategy, and that he may have been experiencing difficulties in determining the spatial orientation and layout of the materials. A second, left-hand trial, albeit markedly impaired, revealed the positive practice effect that is anticipated on subsequent trials. David's third trial (employing both hands) yielded a further small practice effect, but remained markedly impaired. His incidental memory for the shapes of the forms used on this test was essentially normal.

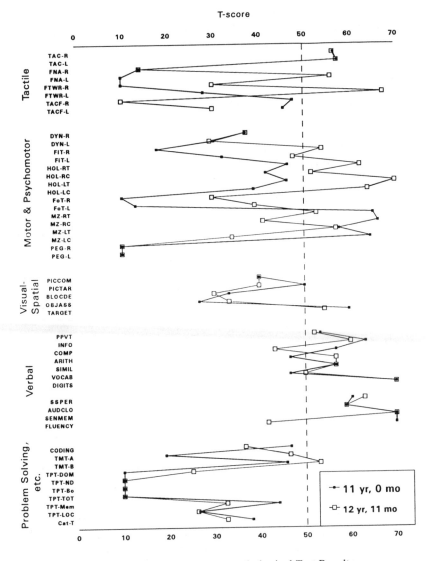

Figure 6.2. Summary of David's Neuropsychological Test Results

NOTE: Explanations of abbreviations: *Tactile:* TAC-R, tactile-perceptual abilities, right hand; TAC-L, tactile-perceptual abilities, left hand; FNA-R, finger agnosia, right hand; FNA-L, finger agnosia, left hand; FTWR-R, fingertip number-writing, right hand; FTWR-L, fingertip number-writing, left hand; TACF-R, tactile-forms recognition, right hand; TACF-L, tactile-forms recognition, left hand.

Motor & Psychomotor: DYN-R, dynamometer (strength of grip), right hand; DYN-L, dynamometer (strength of grip), left hand; FiT-R, finger tapping, right hand; FiT-L, finger tapping, left hand; HOT-RT, Graduated Holes Test, time, right hand; HOL-RC, Graduated Holes Test, contact, right hand;

Ability to recall the proper spatial locations of the objects in a freehand drawing of the formboard, however, was markedly impaired. This finding is consistent with previous results suggesting deficits in spatial analysis, perceptual-organizational abilities, and visual imagery.

No compelling evidence of auditory imperception or suppression was noted. His performances on auditory analysis tasks involving the ability to blend speech sounds to form words, identify the graphic counterparts of novel speech sounds, and attend to and discriminate rhythmic auditory patterns were above average. His performances in the aggregate were indicative of generally well-developed auditory perceptual capacities.

David's short-term recall for a series of digits and his ability to recall and reproduce verbatim sentences of gradually increasing length were above average. His ability to generate words on the basis of phonemic cues was also well developed, while his performance on a screening test assessing the symbolic and communicative aspects of language yielded no clear evidence of anything approaching an aphasic deficit.

Administration of a standardized measure of intellectual abilities (WISC-R) yielded a Verbal IQ of 107. Subtest scaled scores within this section of the WISC-R ranged from lows of 9 on tests of word knowledge and "mental" numerical reasoning (Vocabulary and Arithmetic) to a high of 19 on the Digit Span subtest (a measure involving sustained attention and short-term recall). His fund of general knowledge, ability to make independent social judgments, and verbal associative reasoning capacities all appeared to be relatively strong. David earned a standard score equivalent of 105, a centile ranking of 63, and an age equivalency of 11 years, 10 months on the PPVT-R, a measure of

---

HOL-LT, Graduated Holes Test, time, left hand; HOL-LC, Graduated Holes Test, contact, left hand; MZ-RT, Maze Test, time, right hand; MZ-RC, Maze Test, contact, right hand; MZ-LT, Maze Test, time, left hand; MZ-LC, Maze Test, contact, left hand; PEG-R, Grooved Pegboard, right hand; PEG-L, Grooved Pegboard, left hand.

Visual-Spatial: PICCOM, WISC-R Picture Completion; PICTAR, WISC-R Picture Arrangement; BLOCDE, WISC-R Block Design; OBJASS, WISC-R Object Assembly; TARGET, Target Test.

Verbal: PPVT, Peabody Picture Vocabulary Test; INFO, WISC-R Information; COMP, WISC-R Comprehension; ARITH, WISC-R Arithmetic; SIMIL, WISC-R Similarities; VOCAB, WISC-R Vocabulary; DIGITS, WISC-R Digit Span; SSPER, Speech-Sounds Perception Test; AUDCLO, Auditory Closure Test; SENMEM, Sentence Memory Test; FLUENCY, Verbal Fluency Test.

Problem Solving, Etc.: CODING, WISC-R Coding; TMT-A, Trail Making Test, Part A; TMT-B, Trail Making Test, Part B; TPT-Dom, Tactual Performance Test, dominant hand; TPT-ND, Tactual Performance Test, nondominant hand; TPT-Bo, Tactual Performance Test, both hands; TPT-TOT, Tactual Performance Test, total; TPT-Mem, Tactual Performance Test, memory; TOT-LOC, Tactual Performance Test, location; Cat-T, Category Test.

TABLE 6.2 Summary of David's Test Results at 11 Years, 0 Months and 12 Years, 11 Months

	Testing 1 (11 yrs, 0 mo)	Testing 2 (12 yrs, 11 mo)
WISC-R		
VIQ	107	106
PIQ	78	72
FSIQ	92	88
Underlining (no. of each)		
Superior	1	1
Average	3	3
Borderline	1	1
Mild	2	5
Moderate	5	1
Severe	1	2
Speed Subtest	Moderate	Borderline
WRAT-R (grade/centile)		
Reading	8+/95	12+/99
Spelling	8+/98	12+/95
Arithmetic	4/21	9/68
PIC-R (T score)		
Lie	45	42
F	69	71
Defensiveness	41	37
Adjustment	65	79

receptive word knowledge. In summary, his performances suggested that David's verbal reception and comprehension, verbal production, and (simple) verbal conceptual reasoning skills all appeared to be reasonably well developed.

A cluster of performance inefficiencies was evident, however, on measures of visual-perceptual and visual-spatial capacities. In addition to the difficulties noted earlier on tests of more complex visual-motor abilities (including measures of speeded fine eye-hand coordination, static motor steadiness, and graphomotor execution), he experienced considerable difficulty on measures of visual-discrimination and visual-constructional

TABLE 6.2 Continued

	Testing 1 (11 yrs, 0 mo)	Testing 2 (12 yrs, 11 mo)
Achievement	57	74
Intellectual Screening	72	100
Development	65	82
Somatic Concern	67	42
Depression	81	51
Family Relations	47	43
Delinquency	59	55
Withdrawal	76	65
Anxiety	79	48
Psychosis	112	92
Hyperactivity	31	39
Social Skills	67	77

	Standard Score	Centile	Age-Equivalent Score
VABS (at 11 yrs only)			
Communication	61	< 1	7 yr, 2 mo
Daily Living	27	< 1	4 yr, 6 mo
Socialization	54	< 1	4 yr, 6 mo
Motor		< 1	3 yr, 7 mo
Adaptive Behavior Composite	44	< 1	4 yr, 11 mo

functioning. For example, his performances were consistently poor on a task requiring the rapid identification and underlining of target stimuli interspersed amongst various other distractor items. A qualitative analysis of his performance on this task revealed that his responses improved on items on which he was able to employ a verbally mediated problem-solving strategy.

In a similar manner, David's performance was markedly impaired on a test requiring him to follow a sequence of numerical cues to complete a visual-spatial design. His performance was within normal limits, however, on a related test requiring him to alternate between alphabetic and numeric cues in order to negotiate the visual-spatial array. This discrepancy may reflect some ability on his part to employ verbal strategies to guide his search on the latter task. He was also noted to perform in an average fashion on a task involving the graphic reproduction of sequences of visual stimuli.

A Performance IQ of 78 was in evidence on the WISC-R. Although David exhibited average performances on tasks involving the ability to comprehend a story as told in pictures and to associate symbols to their appropriate numerical counterparts (Picture Arrangement and Coding subtest scaled scores of 10 and 9, respectively), he encountered appreciable difficulties on tasks requiring him to construct abstract visual-spatial designs out of colored blocks and to arrange "puzzle-like" parts into meaningful patterns (Block Design and Object Assembly subtest scaled scores of 5 and 3, respectively). Low-average to mildly impaired performance was in evidence on a task involving sensitivity to fine visual detail (Picture Completion subtest scaled score of 7).

Assessment of David's academic skills (as measured by the Wide Range Achievement Test-Revised) yielded grade equivalent scores approximately 3½ years above chronological age expectation in the areas of written spelling and single-word reading. His performance in mechanical arithmetic, however, was considerably poorer. He achieved standard score equivalents of 124, 131, and 88 on the Reading, Spelling, and Arithmetic subtests, respectively. These scores corresponded to age centile rankings of 95, 98, and 21, respectively. This youngster also earned a reading comprehension age-equivalent score of 8.4 on the Peabody Individual Achievement Test (Dunn & Markwardt, 1970), a performance that ranks in the 55th centile of children his age. Although this performance is within the average range, it represents a relative weakness in reading comprehension as compared to his extremely well-developed word recognition capacities.

Relative weaknesses in comprehension were also reflected in a short story David wrote as part of the assessment. His "story" was simply a listing of facts about family members. Although the form and syntax of the sentences was appropriate, there was no developed story line or "meaning" evident in his composition. Analysis of his performance suggested deficits in the pragmatic dimensions of written language and a paucity of content.

David experienced considerable difficulty on the Category Test (a measure of problem-solving and hypothesis-testing skills). This finding was consistent with other test results suggesting that David manifests

an information processing deficit involving nonverbal concept formation and reasoning. He was noted to perform especially poorly on the
last subtest of the Category Test, a measure involving the capacity to
recall and benefit from prior nonverbal problem-solving experiences.
A personality questionnaire (PIC-R) completed by this youngster's
mother indicated that David was manifesting a number of emotional,
social, and behavioral difficulties. She described him as socially isolated, depressed, anxious, and withdrawn. She appeared to be particularly concerned by his poor social adjustment, flattened affect, and lack
of effective academic and pragmatic adaptive skills. To obtain further
information regarding his adaptive skills, the mother also completed the
Vineland Adaptive Behavior Scale (Sparrow, Balla, & Cicchetti, 1984).
Parental responses to this inventory yielded an Adaptive Behavior
Composite scaled score of 44, a performance that ranks below the .1
centile. Standard score (centile rankings) equivalents of 61 (.5), 27 (less
than .1), and 54 (.1) were noted on the Communication, Daily Living
Skills, and Socialization Domains, respectively. David's adaptive capacities were, in the aggregate, characterized as "low."

Summary, Impression, and Recommendations

From a neurocognitive perspective, this youngster was noted to
manifest significant cognitive, behavioral, and neuropsychological deficits. He demonstrated moderate to marked bilateral tactile perceptual
and psychomotor impairments, and his visual-spatial and nonverbal
problem-solving capacities appeared to be especially compromised. It
is probable that this cluster of neuropsychological performance deficits
underlie the difficulties that he experienced in mechanical arithmetic,
as well as in the area of social adaptation.

A qualitative analysis of his mechanical arithmetic errors revealed an
admixture of procedural, spatial organizational, and judgment and reasoning errors. It was clear that David experienced very marked difficulties in
nonverbal concept formation, strategy generation, and hypothesis testing,
as exemplified by his impaired levels of performance on both the
Category and Tactual Performance Tests. His problems in benefiting
from informational feedback were especially evident on both of these
tests. Inasmuch as one's ability to interact successfully in social situations depends on a capacity to benefit from similar experience in the
past, we would expect that David's neuropsychological deficits in this
area have compromised his ability to learn appropriate social behavior.
These difficulties would be exacerbated by his visual-spatial deficits,

which might affect his ability to perceive and integrate a variety of social cues, such as facial expressions and subtle gestures.

In general, David's auditory perceptual and verbal skills appeared to be relatively well developed. He exhibited a well-developed appreciation for the phonological and/or acoustical structure of language, and his short-term memory for verbal material was excellent. These particular neurocognitive strengths likely contributed to his superior performance in single-word reading and spelling tasks. Although reading comprehension capacities appeared to be age-appropriate, they were significantly weaker than his word-analysis skills. Although single-word reading becomes automatized as the result of well-developed auditory analysis skills, the analysis of novel ideas as well as formulations relating to the content, organization, and synthesis of concepts are hampered by dysfunctional problem-solving capacities. The concept formation and problem-solving difficulties that David experienced are likely also to extend into other realms of his academic development. School subjects that involve logical nonverbal reasoning abilities (e.g., many aspects of natural science), as well as advanced levels of mathematics (calculus and geometry) would be expected to be quite difficult for him.

Because of the nature and severity of this youngster's neurocognitive impairments, it was not expected that his academic and social difficulties would improve spontaneously. As outlined in the Appendix, it was suggested to school personnel that David would most likely benefit from methods of teaching that were primarily verbal in nature. He would also be expected to do reasonably well in the areas of educational content that are primarily verbal in nature, that can be studied and learned in a rote fashion, and that depend primarily upon verbal memory for the demonstration of levels of learning. In contrast, David may well do relatively poorer in areas such as mathematics and science. Indeed, it is expected that he would perform least well in any academic area that places a premium upon concept formation, strategy generation, hypothesis testing, and adaptive problem solving. Specific academic remedial suggestions included the implementation of a parts-to-whole teaching approach, utilization of remedial "crutches" such as handheld calculators and computer-related devices, continual promoting of his reading comprehension capacities, and visual-motor integration skill development. The latter may involve the child as much as possible in skill level or appropriate physical education experiences. Graphomotor tasks should also be executed under the auspices of concrete, structural aids such as a coordinate system or graph paper.

Socioemotionally, it was thought that counseling would prove to be of some assistance in improving David's social adjustment and in alleviating his sense of isolation and dysphoria. Given David's well-developed verbal capacities, he may benefit from a therapeutic approach in which concepts, directions, suggestions, and procedures are generated in a redundant verbal manner. We suggested it would be helpful to have him paraphrase such material to be certain he has comprehended it adequately. A cognitive verbal approach that focuses upon developing his use of self-instruction or "self-vocalization" was thought to be of some assistance in compensating for deficits in nonverbal problem solving. He might, for example, be taught to identify and label the relevant aspects of problematic tasks or interpersonal situations and to develop appropriate strategies. Similarly, cognitive-behavioral interventions might be effective in reducing his feelings of depression. It seemed clear that he should be encouraged to participate in structured and supervised group activities as a means of improving his social adaptation. Role-playing of appropriate responses to recurrent social situations, as well as training in how to recognize various facial expressions, postures, gestures, and "body language" were felt to be appropriate.

Finally, it was recommended that some time be spent developing David's self-care skills. David appeared, for example, to be capable of learning to bathe without assistance, to select clothes and dress himself, and to begin to care for his health. Similarly, he might be encouraged to assist with an increasing range of chores and tasks around the home. It was thought that attempts should be made to develop his skills in telling time and in appreciating the passage of time, as well as in his ability to understand and manage personal money (such as an allowance). Efforts to develop skills that would enable David to function more effectively as an independent adult were also recommended.

Second Assessment

This youngster was seen for neuropsychological reevaluation approximately 2 years after his first assessment, at the age of 12 years, 11 months. In the aggregate, the results of this follow-up examination revealed a pattern of neurocognitive strengths and weaknesses that was remarkably similar to the findings on his initial neuropsychological testing. That is to say, David continued to exhibit a very evident pattern of impaired visual-spatial-organizational skills, eye-hand coordination difficulties, tactile perceptual deficits, and higher level nonverbal concept-formation difficulties, within a context of some well-developed, automatic, rote verbal skills. From a socioemotional perspective, he was characterized as exhibiting behavior features marked by depression, withdrawal, and extreme difficulties in social skills. Although some improvement had been noted in his mechanical arithmetic skills, his performance in this area remained relatively weaker than his word-recognition and spelling competencies.

Although clearly not diagnostic of any active neuropathological condition, this youngster's particular profile of neuropsychological results is often seen in children who are suffering from significant impairment in skills and abilities ordinarily thought to be subserved primarily by systems within the right cerebral hemisphere. In addition, subcortical and diffuse white matter dysfunction is often found to be implicated in such cases. This profile would not be consistent with the presence of an acute neurologic disease; rather, this pattern of skills, abilities, and deficiencies is most often seen in children suffering from a chronic, developmental disability: in this case, NLD.

Discussion

The principal point to be made in this case is that David's pattern of neuropsychological test results in conjunction with his academic and social features reflect the developmental presentation of the NLD syndrome. The ramifications of this particular type of learning disability are far reaching, usually affecting every aspect of academic and social life. As such, the therapeutic programs necessary to handle these difficulties are always quite complex and need to be quite comprehensive and integrated. Specific avenues to pursue in the therapeutic management of NLD children have been discussed in detail elsewhere (Rourke, 1989) and are continued in the Appendix.

The formulation of treatment strategies with children with NLD is based, in part, on a model of brain functioning that implicates the involvement of white matter disease or dysfunction in its manifestations. This is of both theoretical and clinical importance in selecting the appropriate "mode" of intervention. For example, the earlier in development that white matter disease occurs, the more efficacious it would be to utilize a treatment approach that attacks the deficits. This notion is predicated on the assumption that such an approach would serve to stimulate the functioning of the remaining white matter in order to foster the development of centers of gray matter. On the other hand, the longer the syndrome persists, and the later its manifestations, the more likely it is that compensatory techniques will prove to be efficacious in the pursuits of a therapeutic nature.

In view of the particular pattern of neuropsychological strengths and deficiencies exhibited by children with NLD—their difficulties in benefiting from nonverbal experiences, their unusual reliance on language as a primary tool for adaptation, the confusion of their parents and other caretakers concerning the nature or significance of their condition, and the inappropriate expectations of such children by all concerned—many of the initial aspects of the treatment program are focused on the perceptions of the parents and other caretakers. Although not all children who exhibit the NLD syndrome have identical developmental histories or behave exactly as outlined above, the similarities in behavior outcomes for such children are remarkably similar.

At the same time, it is clear that the ability of the child's primary caretakers to understand his or her deficiencies early in life and to generate appropriate expectations for such a child is an important factor in determining the degree to which he or she will exhibit maladaptive or atypical behavior in later childhood. Furthermore, thoughtful guidance from the child's parents and specialized forms of treatment outside of the home situation are also important determinants of general prognosis.

Finally, the degree of neuropsychological impairment would appear to be an important consideration. Children whose abilities are significantly impaired and who exhibit the full constellation of neuropsychological deficits that are the hallmarks of the NLD syndrome are those who would appear to be most at risk for maladaptive consequences.

The rehabilitation considerations for children with NLD that are contained in the Appendix are somewhat detailed because we hope that this will (a) increase the likelihood that practitioners will consider them as treatment options and (b) serve as a model for treatment programs for other subtypes of LD that, like this one, should be subject to empirical tests. Unfortunately, it is seldom found that children with NLD are involved in educational or other programs that are appropriate for their special learning needs. This is particularly unfortunate because, if treatment is not instituted fairly early on all academic and behavioral fronts, the prognosis tends to be quite bleak.

CASE 3: JEFFREY (OUTPUT DISORDER)

In addition to LD characterized primarily by (a) disorders of linguistic functioning, and (b) disorders of nonverbal functioning, a third type of learning disability is characterized by outstanding problems in the output of information (see Chapter 5). Although word-finding and verbal expressive problems are cardinal features of this subtype of LD, there are added problems of deficient output in the writing of words and written arithmetic. From a developmental perspective, rather severe problems in oral and written output are prominent in early school years with marked advances in word recognition, word decoding, and reading comprehension evident in the middle school years. Written work remains poor, as does the capacity to deliver verbal descriptions and answers to questions. Such children are often characterized as having acting-out disorders in early school years. They are also at risk for social withdrawal and depression. This may develop into full-blown externalized and/or internalized forms of psychopathology if management by the child's principal caretakers is inappropriate.

Background and Relevant History

This boy of almost 8 years was referred at the direction of his school psychologist for evaluation of poor handwriting and possible fine motor coordination problems. It was the mother's impression that Jeffrey was slow in the development of his gross and fine motor skills. He was noted to experience significant difficulties in handwriting throughout his early kindergarten placement, although he impressed his teachers as being especially knowledgeable in the areas of science and number and letter identification. Although he was not described as exhibiting any noteworthy behavioral problems during his early kindergarten years, he reportedly began to exhibit features of motoric restlessness, verbal disruptiveness, inattentiveness, distractibility, and impulsivity over the subsequent 1 to 2 years. In addition to his difficulties in handwriting and coordination, problems in mechanical arithmetic reportedly surfaced.

By way of developmental background, this youngster was reported to be the product of a full-term, normal cephalic delivery. Birth weight was 9 lb. 13 oz. There were no significant gestational complications reported, and this youngster's immediate postnatal growth and development proceeded normally. The acquisition of motor milestones was characterized by the ability to sit alone by 8 months, stand by 12 months, initiate his first steps at 13 months, and walk unaided by 17 months of age. He uttered his first words by 9 months, spoke in simple phrases by 15 months, and exhibited reasonably good sentence structure by 2 years of age. His medical history revealed that he has experienced asthmatic-related problems since 13 months of age for which he had been treated with a variety of medications, including Ventolin, Intal, and Slophyllin. Psychosocial history revealed Jeffrey to be the youngest in a biological sibship of two. There was no history of academic, behavioral, or medical problems in Jeffrey's older sister. Jeffrey's mother completed an advanced level of academic instruction (MA degree), and his biological father completed 13 years of formal education. There was no history of any LD, language impairment, or ADHD-like problems in any other immediate family members. At the time of this assessment, the home environment was described as being stable and supportive.

Behavioral Observations During the Examination

There was a gradual progression of declining attentional capacities and increased motoric restlessness as this youngster moved from the morning to the afternoon session of testing. He was rather verbally precocious, and he sometimes distracted himself by talking and asking questions during the execution of a task. Although he was not necessarily oppositional, he was somewhat manipulative. He held his pencil very close to the lead and he maintained his eyes very close to the paper when engaged in graphomotor tasks. Several letter reversals were noted, and he tended to press quite firmly with his pencil on graphomotor tasks. On certain drawing tasks, he was noted to switch his preferred hand in the middle of the task.

When asked to count his fingers, he encountered difficulty maintaining the proper association between his verbal and finger display responses, often needing to touch his fingers against his face when counting. Physically, significant nasal congestion and labored breathing were noted as well as mild tremulousness in his upper extremities.

All things considered, it was felt that these test results represented a fairly reliable and valid reflection of his neurocognitive status.

Test Results and Interpretations

Jeffrey's test results are summarized in Figure 6.3 and Table 6.3. An examination for lateral dominance suggested that this youngster was exclusively right-handed, right-footed, and left-eyed. Strength of grip

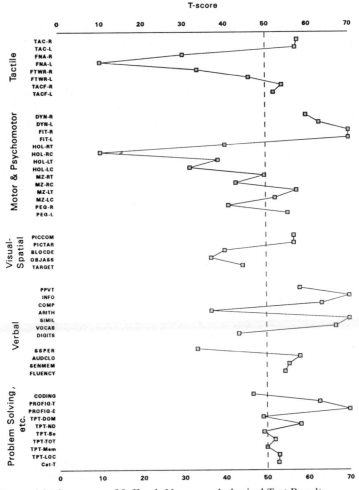

Figure 6.3. Summary of Jeffrey's Neuropsychological Test Results

NOTE: Explanations of abbreviations: *Tactile:* TAC-R, tactile-perceptual abilities, right hand; TAC-L, tactile-perceptual abilities, left hand; FNA-R, finger agnosia, right hand; FNA-L, finger agnosia, left hand; FTWR-R, fingertip number-writing, right hand; FTWR-L, fingertip number-writing, left hand; TACF-R, tactile-forms recognition, right hand; TACF-L, tactile-forms recognition, left hand.

Motor & Psychomotor: DYN-R, dynamometer (strength of grip), right hand; DYN-L, dynamometer (strength of grip), left hand; FiT-R, finger tapping, right hand; FiT-L, finger tapping, left hand; HOL-RT, Graduated Holes Test, time, right hand; HOL-RC, Graduated Holes Test, contact, right hand; HOL-LT, Graduated Holes Test, time, left hand; HOL-LC, Graduated Holes Test, contact, left hand; MZ-RT, Maze Test, time, right hand; MZ-RC, Maze Test, contact, right hand; MZ-LT, Maze Test, time, left hand; MZ-LC, Maze Test, contact, left hand; PEG-R, Grooved Pegboard, right hand; PEG-L, Grooved Pegboard, left hand.

Visual-Spatial: PICCOM, WISC-R Picture Completion; PICTAR, WISC-R Picture Arrangement; BLOCDE, WISC-R Block Design; OBJASS, WISC-R Object Assembly; TARGET, Target Test.

was average bilaterally, and his performance was well above average with each hand on a finger oscillation task. Performance on a kinetic motor steadiness examination was acceptable with each hand, but he did exhibit some mild problems bilaterally on motor steadiness testing within the static disposition. His performance on a speeded fine eye-hand coordination task was mildly slowed with the right hand and average with the left hand.

There was no compelling evidence for any simple tactile impercep-tion or suppression. Finger agnosia examination yielded a moderately impaired performance with the right hand and a markedly impaired performance with the left hand. He encountered some mild problems with his right hand on finger dysgraphesthesia testing, while left-handed performance on this measure was average. Astereognosis ex-amination yielded error-free performances bilaterally. He also exhibited average performances on all three trials (right hand, left hand, conjoint hand) of one relatively complex tactually guided problem-solving task (involving tactile form discrimination, manual dexterity, and haptic kinesthetic feedback). Both incidental learning and topo-graphical memory performances on this task were average.

A measure of visual acuity yielded performances of 20/50 and 20/70 with the right and left eye, respectively. Tests for visual field defects were negative. Both right- and left-hand name-printing performances were characterized by crude letter formations, variable inter-letter spac-ing, and mild kinetic tremulousness. His printing performances bor-dered on dysgraphia, and his drawings of simple geometric configurations (including a square, Greek cross, and triangle) suggested some mild motor/graphomotor difficulties (see Figure 6.4). His per-formance on the Beery Developmental Test of Visual Motor Integration yielded a standard score of 72, a centile ranking of 3, and an age equivalency of 5 years, 2 months. He exhibited a low-average level of

---

Verbal: PPVT, Peabody Picture Vocabulary Test; INFO, WISC-R Information; COMP, WISC-R Com-prehension; ARITH, WISC-R Arithmetic; SIMIL, WISC-R Similarities; VOCAB, WISC-R Vocabulary; DIGITS, WISC-R Digit Span; SSPER, Speech-Sounds Perception Test; AUDCLO, Auditory Closure Test; SENMEM, Sentence Memory Test; FLUENCY, Verbal Fluency Test.

Problem Solving, Etc.: CODING, WISC-R Coding; PROFIG-T, Progressive Figures, Time; PROFIG-E, Progressive Figures; Errors. TPT-Dom, Tactual Performance Test, dominant hand; TPT-ND, Tactual Performance Test, nondominant hand; TPT-Bo, Tactual Performance Test, both hands; TPT-TOT, Tactual Performance Test, total; TPT-Mem, Tactual Performance Test, memory; TOT-LOC, Tactual Performance Test, location; Cat-T, Category Test.

TABLE 6.3   Summary of Jeffrey's Test Results at 7 Years, 10 Months

	Testing at 7 yrs, 10 mo
WISC-R	
VIQ	123
PIQ	93
FSIQ	110
Underlining (no. of each)	
Superior	2
Average	6
Borderline	0
Mild	3
Moderate	3
Severe	0
Speed Subtest	Average
WRAT-R (grade/centile)	
Reading	1/18
Spelling	1/.8
Arithmetic	2/47
PIC-R (*T* score)	
Lie	30
F	69
Defensiveness	41
Adjustment	65
Achievement	68
Intellectual Screening	107
Development	69
Somatic Concern	91
Depression	50
Family Relations	53
Delinquency	40
Withdrawal	47
Anxiety	63
Psychosis	56
Hyperactivity	66
Social Skills	47

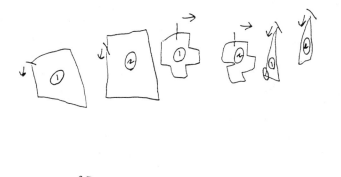

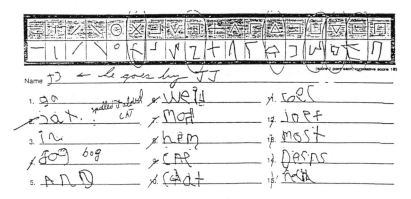

Figure 6.4. Examples of Jeffrey's Drawing and Printing

performance on a task involving the ability to remember and reproduce graphically sequences of visual stimuli, while his performance was mildly impaired (Perceptual Quotient = 87, Perceptual Age = 6 years) on the Motor Free Visual Perceptual Test. Finally, performance on the Underlining Test (Rourke & Petrauskas, 1977; a series of subtests involving the rapid underlining of various types of verbal and nonverbal stimuli interspersed among various distractor items) was characterized by declines in performance as subtest stimuli increased in verbal and sequential complexity.

This youngster exhibited a Performance IQ of 93 on the WISC-R. Subtest performances within this section of the WISC-R ranged from mildly impaired on tasks involving the ability to construct abstract visual-spatial designs out of colored blocks and to arrange "puzzle-like" parts into meaningful patterns (Block Design and Object Assembly subtest scaled scores of 7 and 6, respectively) to high-average performances on tasks involving the ability to identify the missing parts in pictures of commonly encountered objects and to comprehend a story as told in pictures (Picture Completion and Picture Arrangement subtest scaled scores of 12). An associative learning task involving speed and accuracy of symbolic transcription yielded an average performance (Coding subtest scaled score of 9).

There was no indication of any simple auditory imperception or suppression, and there was no indication of any auditory acuity deficits on a Pure Tone Sweep Hearing Test. He encountered some mild problems on phoneme-grapheme matching and phonemic discrimination/segmentation tasks, yet his performance was average on acoustical blending and phonemically and categorically cued verbal fluency measures. Immediate recall for sequences of digits (4 forward, 3 backward) was low-average, while he exhibited an average performance in his immediate recall for sentences of gradually increasing length. He also exhibited high-average immediate recall, long-term storage, long-term retrieval, and consistent long-term retrieval scores on the Buschke Selective Reminding Test (a task involving the ability to learn a series of unrelated words).

His performances were largely unremarkable on those portions of a brief screening test designed to measure some basic symbolic and communicational aspects of language. He exhibited a standard score of 112, a centile ranking of 78, and an age equivalency of 9 years, 1 month on the PPVT-R, while performance on the Expressive One Word Picture Vocabulary Test yielded an IQ of 130, centile ranking of 98, and mental age equivalency of 10 years, 11 months.

A Verbal IQ of 123 was in evidence on the WISC-R. His weakest performances occurred on the Arithmetic (subtest scaled score of 6) and Digit Span (subtest scaled score of 8) subtests, a pattern commonly associated with concentration and attentional deployment difficulties. On the other hand, his performances were quite superior on tasks designed to assess fund of factual and functional word knowledge, understanding of appropriate social mores and customs, and verbal abstraction facility (Information, Vocabulary, Comprehension, and Similarities subtest scaled scores of 17, 15, 14, and 17, respectively).

An average performance was in evidence on the Category Test (Reitan & Davison, 1974; a problem-solving task involving some degree of concept formation, hypothesis testing, and the ability to benefit from positive and negative informational feedback), and he was quite adept at negotiating his way through a visual-spatial array while shifting between size and shape cues in an alternate fashion.

Brief academic achievement testing with the WRAT-R yielded the following standard score equivalents: Reading (word recognition), 86; Spelling, 60; Arithmetic, 99. Based on his chronological age, these scores corresponded to centile rankings (grade equivalents) of 18 (1M), .8 (P1), and 47 (2B), respectively. His performance on the Spelling subtest of the WRAT-R was characterized by several distortions in his copying of simple symbols, dysgraphic print, and evidence of phonemic imperceptions and substitutions. He tended to utilize a "best guess" strategy based on the most salient visual characteristics in his reading of novel, unfamiliar words.

A series of behavioral questionnaires (including the PIC-R) completed by this youngster's mother tended to describe him as exhibiting behavioral features characterized by poor self-confidence, attentional deployment difficulties, impulse control problems, oppositionality (subsuming characteristics of quarrelsomeness, stubbornness, and defiance), motoric disinhibition, immaturity, limited frustration tolerance, and peer disruptiveness. Somatization tendencies were also described, as well as tendencies toward lying, cheating, and denial of blame.

Summary, Impressions, and Recommendations

There were many features to this youngster's psychometric protocol to suggest that his visual-motor/perceptual-motor/visual-constructive capacities were somewhat underdeveloped. This was particularly noteworthy on tasks of a graphomotor nature and was also manifested on complex visual-sequencing tasks and speeded fine eye-hand coordination measures. Visual perceptual/discrimination capacities, on the other hand, appeared to be relatively better developed, suggesting that this youngster's problem was more of an intersensory/intermodal rather than intramodal processing limitation. Associated difficulties were noted in certain areas of haptic perceptual functioning, including those involving the adequate localization and recognition of certain types of tactile input.

Equally impressive in this test protocol were this youngster's strong neurocognitive performances. Performance on many auditory-verbal and language-related measures, for example, was at—and, in several cases, above—age expectancy levels. He possessed an extraordinarily well-developed fund of functional word knowledge, memory capacities appeared to be functionally intact, and verbal abstraction and/or deductive reasoning skills appeared to be reasonably well developed.

There were several problematic aspects to this youngster's behavioral functioning. His ability to deploy his attention (especially for any sustained period of time) seemed to be lacking, and a certain degree of motor disinhibition was noted during the clinical exam. In addition to somatization tendencies, the results of a number of behavioral questionnaires completed by this youngster's mother suggested the presence of rather significant concentration, motoric restlessness, impulse control, and frustration tolerance difficulties. Some degree of behavioral resistance also appeared to be present within the home environment; this subsumed characteristics of stubbornness, denial of responsibility, rebelliousness, and uncooperativeness. The sources of many of this youngster's behavioral problems were not at all clear. Although children with similar sorts of neurocognitive processing limitations are often described by a multiplicity of labels (that include disorganized, impulsive, distractible, and overactive), similar behavioral manifestations have also been found to be correlated with severe asthma-related problems. To complicate matters further, this youngster's behavioral presentation was felt to fit many of the behavioral criteria commonly associated with an Attention Deficit/Hyperactivity Disturbance.

It was felt that the sorts of neurocognitive impairments exhibited by this youngster were likely to interfere with the smooth development of his academic competencies. Providing him with some degree of special education assistance was felt to be a necessary, if not critical, treatment recommendation. In addition to concentrating on visual-motor skill development, it was felt that some time should be spent improving this youngster's internal organizational capacities, sequencing abilities, and impulsivity and distractibility tendencies. Although it was suggested that cognitive-behavioral interventions might be helpful in dealing with this youngster's disruptive behavior, it was pointed out to school personnel that several studies (e.g., Barkley, 1990) have demonstrated that such approaches should be integrated with the teaching styles of the child's teacher for use in day-to-day exchanges, rather than taught in formal, one-to-one sessions outside of school. As an adjunct to classroom management, it was suggested that the parents become involved in some type of parent management program to deal with this youngster's oppositional tendencies. Integrating school- and home-based management programs was stressed in order to facilitate consistency and generalization across settings.

Although this youngster was noted to encounter some mild problems on auditory analysis tasks involving the correspondences between phonemes and graphemes, it was felt that the psychomotor dimensions of his writing difficulties were contaminating this process somewhat during spelling tasks in particular, largely as a function of an inability to decipher his own written script. In this regard, it was suggested that school personnel may wish to experiment with more informal "by-pass strategies" when the task demands require much in the way of graphomotor output. In this regard, it is interesting to note that the mother of this youngster reported that Jeffrey was quite capable of generating creative and sophisticated compositions under oral production conditions, and yet school personnel reported that he had great difficulty generating stories when he has to write this same information down on paper.

Given these facts, we suggested that school personnel might wish to consider experimenting with the utilization of word processing, typewriting, and dictaphone systems in doing tasks of this nature. The use of ditto notes (with key words left blank), additional time to complete work, and possibly supplementary oral quizzes were thought to be beneficial for him.

In addition to these by-pass strategies, exercises that aimed to improve his visuomotor integration skill development were recommended. Drawing and tracing activities whereby the child begins with simple designs that gradually add complexity and increased demand for greater accuracy were recommended. For example, having the child draw numerous lines from left to right (e.g., to a vertical line on the right), single continuous circles (changing the size of the circles, varying the speed, and drawing circles with both hands), or a series of continuous circles or cursive letters (*I*s, *L*s, *E*s, etc.) could form an important base for improvement of written expression skills.

It has also been suggested in the literature (Laslo & Broderick, 1991) that printing is a more difficult task than cursive writing. This stems from the notion that discrete units are less adequately reproduced than

are continuous patterns constructed of the same units, due to the increased planning demand from continuous to discrete patterns. In other
words, cursive script tends to lend itself to the rapid development of an
automatized motor skill more so than does printing. In the case of this
youngster, printing may be an unnecessary step, especially if cursive
writing can improve his productions.

Discussion

In contrast to linguistically impaired children who are generally
found to have difficulty in accessing a normal store of verbal associations in the context of adequately developed writing skills, this case
illustrates a distinct subtype of LD marked by problems with written
expression and/or graphomotor execution. Performance under conditions
of speeded fine eye-hand coordination is somewhat deficient, as is the
ability to generate verbal productions under highly rule-governed conditions (despite marked advances in word knowledge or vocabulary).

In many ways, this case is similar to children who have been described
as exhibiting a "developmental output failure" (Levine, Oberklaid, &
Meltzer, 1981; Seigel & Feldman, 1982). Common findings among
this group of children include problems with fine motor dexterity or
speed of output, verbal expression, configuration retrieval memory,
sequential memory, finger agnosia, and selective attention. Difficulty with handwriting, of course, represents a cardinal feature of
these children.

In the earlier phases of their academic career these children may
not necessarily be perceived as encountering difficulties in the acquisition
of basic academic skills, but the necessity for rapid and high-volume
written output may precipitate a decline in late elementary and early
high school. These children come to the attention of health care professionals because of recurrent complaints of difficulty in completing assignments, trouble with written work, and organizational problems.

Remediation and rehabilitation for these children is crucial but difficult. Part of this difficulty relates to the impression that persists in the
minds of many involved in the educational process that a child who
reads well could not possibly have any outstanding educational needs.
This being the case, it is seldom found that such children are involved
in educational programs that are appropriate for their special learning
needs. It is not uncommon to find school personnel adopting the position that their chronic failure to complete assigned work is due more to
psychosocial causes (e.g, inappropriate attitudes, environmental cir-

cumstances, or emotional difficulties) than to a subtle developmental problem that impairs productivity.

Because of the difficulties these children encounter with arithmetic, there has been a tendency to view their associated cognitive problems within the same neuropsychological framework of other children with arithmetic disabilities (i.e., an NLD). Although children with output disorders (OD) and children with NLD are similar in many respects, there are fundamental differences between these two subtypes of LD. From a neurocognitive perspective, children with OD do not typically exhibit the same problems in age-appropriate concept formation and problem solving that are especially evident in children with NLD. The principal deficits in linguistic skills relating to the content and pragmatic dimensions of language that are evident in children with NLD are generally not found to exist in children afflicted with OD. Following initial problems with the visuomotor aspects of writing and much practice with a writing instrument, graphomotor skills (for words) are found to reach good to excellent levels in children with NLD. In addition, single-word spelling to dictation skills are found to develop to above-average levels in such children. In the advancing years, the gap between good to excellent single-word reading and spelling and deficient mechanical arithmetic performance widens in the child with NLD: Problems in reading comprehension, especially for novel material, tend to increase in advancing years in these children as well. In contrast, children with OD generally exhibit marked advances in word recognition, word decoding, and reading comprehension in the context of deficient written spelling and mechanical arithmetic performances.

Due to the normal progression of reading skills, children with OD frequently escape detection during their early school years. When the process demands of the academic milieu require more in the way of efficient and effortful writing productivity, however, academic struggles may begin to emerge. While these may involve primarily problems with written work, the additional difficulty of organizing, directing, and orchestrating different aspects of behavioral expression is likely to be manifested.

The principal impediments in remediating this type of LD include (a) a poor appreciation (or, in some cases, unacceptance) by school personnel of the sorts of neuropsychological deficiencies that may account for the child's inability to acquire normal spelling and arithmetic skills, and (b) a failure on the part of the remedial team to implement instructional strategies that tend to be more "compensatory" in nature at a much younger age.

More generally, with respect to the child with LD, a developmental neuropsychological approach is designed to identify patterns of central processing assets and deficits that may predispose a youngster to predictably different patterns of academic LD and social adaptational difficulties. Utilized in concert with the more traditional psychoeducational examination, a rich body of clinically useful descriptive information regarding the youngster's cognitive, academic, behavioral adjustment, and socioemotional functioning can be obtained. As to the issue of remediation, there is no substitute for creative and flexible approaches to the provision of therapeutic aids or crutches. These include the utilization of computers and tape recorders as prosthetic/therapeutic devices; application of alternative test-taking procedures; and modification of written assignments, including reductions in output volume and speed of production. During the child's early junior and high school years, hand calculators could be used to provide the child with a way to check the accuracy of his or her mechanical arithmetic work. This will enable the adolescent to develop at least a functional grasp of common mathematical operations and their applications in everyday life situations.

Clearly, we need to establish whether and to what extent the specificity of LD identification leads to specificity of efficacious treatments. Vapid debates regarding the relative utility of deficit- or compensatory-driven strategies at different stages of development will continue to be the rule until we make considerably more headway in this area. To this end, we need to focus on investigations in which preferred modes of intervention are deduced from models of neuropsychological relationships that have been shown to have concurrent and predictive validity. The work of Bakker and his associates (e.g., Bakker, 1986, 1990; Bakker et al., 1991) is one example of this approach; that of Lyon and associates (e.g., Lyon & Flynn, 1991) is another. Both of these approaches have shown considerable promise and we can expect to see more developments along these lines in the near future.

AFTERWORD

In this book, we have attempted to describe and explain in some detail a particular approach to the understanding, assessment, and treatment of children and adolescents with LD. This neuropsychological modus operandi has taken a considerable amount of time and effort to develop. The payoff, in our view, is that a comprehensive, systematic, and effective approach is emerging from these efforts.

We have emphasized the interplay between basic research on subtyping on the one hand and assessment and intervention strategies on the other. This tack was adopted because it is our strong feeling that this is the manner in which our understanding, assessment, and treatment of children with LD will continue to be enhanced. We view the scientist-practitioner approach to this field to be particularly suited to its current state of development.

As we hope can be seen clearly in this book, our approach to these important issues has been to examine "clinical material" carefully and then to formulate hypotheses about how we might clarify relationships between neuropsychological assets and deficits on the one hand and issues regarding academic and social learning on the other. Steps along the way to this level of understanding necessarily entailed a considerable amount of effort in the subtyping of patterns of neuropsychological assets and deficits as well as the subtyping of patterns of personality functioning exhibited by children and adolescents with LD.

For these and other reasons, we would view narrow experimental approaches to very specific dimensions of learning and psychosocial functioning in children with undifferentiated LD to be counterproductive at this or any other time. Unless and until we have a consensually validated typology of LD, piecemeal research on heterogeneous groups of LD and the practical ramifications that result therefrom will be fragmented, confused, and confusing. Of course, insisting that each child with LD is implacably unique in every way precludes any science of LD and returns us to "square one." Indeed, we view our "subtyping" approach to LD as treading a middle road between narrow experimental, nomothetic approaches and the strictly idiosyncratic viewpoint.

It is clear that the approach to assessment that has emerged from this undertaking and that we have described herein is a complex one. In the hands of an experienced child clinical neuropsychologist we would expect it to be employed in a responsible and efficacious manner. (Guidelines for the training that would qualify one to do this are readily available [Reports of the INS-Division 40 Task Force, 1987].) We would hope that readers who do not now have such expertise will, nevertheless, come to understand this framework and that this understanding will lead to a coherent view of this multifaceted and fascinating field.

Finally, we would note that the interested reader may wish to consult the following works that contain numerous case studies of children, adolescents, and adults with LD: Rourke (1985); Rourke (1989); Rourke (1991); Rourke et al., (1983); Rourke, Fisk, and Strang (1986); Rourke and Fuerst (1991).

APPENDIX:
TREATMENT PROGRAM FOR THE
CHILD WITH NLD

The following is as an example of the sort of treatment program that can emerge from the systematic, comprehensive analysis of children who exhibit a specific subtype of LD. In this case, a program of intervention of the NLD subtype is discussed.

ORGANIZATION OF THE TREATMENT PROGRAM

The following sections of the treatment program are couched in fairly general terms, with an emphasis upon general principles. Our ordinary practice is to present these to the child's principal caretakers and, in the process, make those modifications that are necessary to meet specific individual, family, community, and other individuating factors that are operative in the particular case.

A NOTE REGARDING THE NLD SYNDROME
IN RELATION TO THE TREATMENT PROGRAM

In view of the particular pattern of neuropsychological strengths and deficits exhibited by children with NLD—their difficulties in benefiting from nonverbal experiences, their unusual reliance on language as a primary tool for adaptation, the confusion of their parents and other caretakers concerning the nature or significance of their condition, and the inappropriate expectations of such children by all concerned—much of the initial phases of the treatment program are focused on the perceptions of the parents and other caretakers. Although not all children who exhibit the NLD syndrome have identical developmental histories or behave exactly as outlined in the body of this work, the behavioral outcomes for such children are remarkably similar. At the same time, it is clear that the ability of the child's primary caretakers to understand his or her deficits early in life and to generate appropriate expectations for such a child are important factors in determining the degree to which he or she will exhibit maladaptive or atypical behavior in later childhood. Furthermore, thoughtful guidance from the child's parents and specialized forms of treatment outside of the home situation are also important determinants of general prognosis. Finally, the *degree* of neuropsychological impairment would appear to be an important consideration. Children whose abilities are outstandingly impaired and who exhibit the full constellation of neuropsychological deficits that are the hallmarks of the NLD syndrome are those who would appear to be most at risk for maladaptive consequences.

THE PROGRAM

Outlined below are some common features of an integrated and carefully orchestrated program of intervention that we have found to be helpful for children and adolescents who exhibit the NLD syndrome. This material is an adapted from Strang and Rourke (1985a) and Rourke (1989). The program involves the principal caretakers (parents, teachers, therapists) at every step of the way. For example, one of the first steps in a remediation/habilitation program involves providing the parents with appropriate information concerning the nature and significance of their child's neuropsychological assets and deficits. Often, the child's parents require fairly continuous counseling and support in order to gear their expectations and their parenting methods and techniques to fit the child's most salient developmental needs.

Remediation and habilitation for the child with NLD is crucial but difficult. Part of this difficulty relates to the impression that persists in the minds of many involved in the educational process and others that a child who reads and spells well could not possibly have any outstanding educational needs. This being the case, it is seldom found that such children are involved in educational programs that are appropriate for their special learning needs. This is particularly unfortunate because, if treatment is not instituted fairly early and on all fronts (including academic) in such a child's life, the prognosis tends to be quite bleak. With these remarks as background, the following general principles of intervention are offered. These principles are framed as suggestions to principal caregivers.

1. Observe the Child's Behavior Closely, Especially in Novel or Otherwise Complex Situations

During this potentially informative exercise, focus on what the child does and disregard what the child says. This should help the parent, therapist, and/or teacher to develop a better appreciation of the child's potentially outstanding adaptive deficits and to shape their own cognitive "set" for interventions with the child. One of the most frequent criticisms of remedial intervention programs with this particular type of child is that remedial authorities are unaware of the extent and significance of the child's deficits. Through direct observation under these conditions, it should become apparent that the child is very much in need of a systematic, well-orchestrated program of intervention.

Examples: Arrange for parents to observe their child at play with other children; videotape such interactions or solitary behavior in the classroom; explain the results of well-standardized rating scales of social behavior and other relevant dimensions—for example, NLD Scale (Rourke, 1993); Vineland Adaptive Behavior Scale (Sparrow, Balla, & Cicchetti, 1984)—that are completed by persons who are very familiar with the child.

2. Adopt a Realistic Attitude

Once it has been established that the child's behavior is nonadaptive, particularly in new or otherwise complex situations, one must then be realistic in assessing the import and impact of the child's neuropsychological assets (e.g., "automatic" language skills, rote memory) and deficits (e.g., visual-spatial-organizational skills). In the classroom, for instance, it should be readily apparent that the child's well-developed word-recognition and spelling abilities are not sufficient for him or her to benefit from many forms of formal and informal instruction, especially for those subjects that require visual-spatial-organizational and/or nonverbal problem-solving skills. This being the case, there are really only two educational alternatives: It is necessary either to adopt special procedures for the presentation of material of the latter variety, or to avoid such material altogether. Some suggestions for "special procedures" follow.

3. Teach the Child in a Systematic, "Step-By-Step" Fashion

Whenever possible, use a parts-to-whole verbal teaching approach. As a rule of thumb, the therapist or teacher should take note that, if it is possible to talk about an idea, concept, or procedure in a straightforward fashion, then the child should be able to grasp at least some aspects of the material. On the other hand, if it is not possible to put into words an adequate description of the material to be learned (e.g., as in explaining time concepts), it will probably be quite difficult for the child with NLD to benefit from the instruction.

It should also be kept in mind that the child will learn best when each of the verbal "steps" is in the correct sequence, because of his or her inadequate problem-solving skills and associated organizational difficulties with novel (even linguistically novel) material. A secondary benefit of this teaching approach is that the child is provided with a set of verbal rules than can be written out and then reapplied whenever it is appropriate to do so. This is particularly important for the teaching of mechanical arithmetic operations and procedures.

The principal impediment to engaging in this rather slow and painstaking approach to teaching the child with NLD is the caregiver's (faulty) impression that the child is much more adept and adaptable than is actually the case. This increases the probability that the caregiver will start the program at a level that is too sophisticated for the child, and will proceed at too fast a clip for the information-processing capacities of the child. The child with NLD, on the other hand, tends to respond quite appreciatively and appropriately to an approach that is slow, repetitive, and highly redundant.

4. Encourage the Child to Describe in Detail Important Events That Are Transpiring in His or Her Life

This remedial recommendation applies not only to teaching sessions with the child, but also to any situation in which the child does not seem to appreciate fully the significance of his or her behavior or the behavior of others. For example, when there is an incident on the playground in which the child has encountered interpersonal difficulty, ask the child to explain in detail the events that transpired and what he or she perceives to be the cause of the incident and its effects. Encourage the child to focus on the relevant aspects of the situation. Point out the irrelevancies that are brought up. Through discussion, help the child to become aware of discrepancies between his or her perceptions (regarding the situation in question) and the perceptions of others. In teaching situations, one technique found useful is to encourage the child to "re-teach" the teacher or therapist (or in some situations, teach other children) the procedure or concept that he or she has been taught. This will help to increase the probability that the child has understood the necessary information, that it has been analyzed and integrated, and that it will be applied in future situations.

5. Teach the Child Appropriate Strategies for Dealing With Particularly Troublesome Situations That Occur on a Frequent, Everyday Basis

In many cases, children with NLD do not generate appropriate problem-solving strategies independently because they are unaware of the actual requirements of the situation. At other times, the child may be unable to generate appropriate strategies because this particular type of endeavor requires basic neuropsychological competencies that the child has not developed. For both of these reasons, such children need to be taught appropriate strategies for handling the requirements of frequently occurring troublesome situations. The teacher or therapist will find that the step-by-step requirements for teaching this type of child are quite similar to those that would be employed effectively for much younger children. Once again, it should be emphasized that the most frequent error made by adult caretakers in such situations is to overestimate the capacities of children with NLD to learn and to apply adaptive problem-solving solutions and techniques for coping.

6. Encourage the Generalization of Learned Strategies and Concepts

Although the majority of "normal" children see how one particular strategy or procedure may apply to a number of different situations, and/or how certain concepts may apply to a wide range of topics, the child with NLD usually exhibits difficulties with this form of generalization. For example, it is common to find that, although the child with NLD has been trained assiduously in visual attention and visual tracking skills in the laboratory or therapeutic setting, he or she fails to employ the skills effectively in everyday life (e.g., when it would be propitious to examine some aspects of a person's physical characteristics in order to enhance recognition of that person in the future). It is abundantly clear that the child with NLD not only needs to be taught specific skills in a step-by-step fashion, but also that transitional or generalization skills need to be addressed in an identical manner.

Related to these difficulties is a very persistent and pervasive deficit in the judgment of cause-effect relationships. For example, the child with NLD may not discern, even after hundreds of experiences with a particular event, that there is nascent within it a reasonable and easily inferable causal linkage. The child may not discern, for instance, that there is a causal connection between flipping a light switch and the illumination or termination of illumination of a light fixture. Most often, the child has to be shown quite explicitly that (say) the up position on the light switch signals on, and the down position, off. The vast majority of persons unfamiliar with NLD fail to see that such relationships have to be brought quite explicitly to the child's attention because children with NLD do not make the same sort of inferences regarding cause and effect that are arrived at spontaneously and without difficulty by children not so afflicted.

7. Teach the Child to Refine and Use
Appropriately His or Her Verbal (Expressive) Skills

As has been pointed out previously, it is quite probable that the child with NLD will come to use verbal (expressive) skills much more frequently and for much different reasons than do most children. For example, such a child may repeatedly ask questions as a primary way of gathering information about a new or otherwise complex situation. This may be quite inappropriate for many situations (e.g., of a social nature) in which non-verbal behaviors are much more important for feedback and direction.

The content of the child's verbal responses may also be problematic. A common observation is that the child with NLD may begin to make a reply by directly addressing the question asked, but then gradually drift off into a completely different topic. At the very least, the tangential nature of such utterances has the effect of alienating the listener. Specific training should be undertaken that is directed at "what to say," "how to say," and "when to say" aspects of language as these questions apply to the child's problem areas. As with other aspects of remediation mentioned above, however, there is the problem of generalization of learning in this sort of training exercise. The child with NLD tends not to be flexible and adaptive in the application of learned habits, even when these are in his or her areas of "strength" (i.e., verbal skills).

For these and many other reasons, it is usually necessary to spend considerable time and effort to train the child to stop, look, listen, and weigh alternatives, even in what may appear to the casual observer to be mundane, straightforward situations. Failure to anticipate the consequences of their actions often leads children with NLD to rush into situations where they are very likely to suffer physical and/or psychological harm. Their usual tendency is to avoid such situations after repeated failure and pain. The caregiver's role is to help the child to deal effectively with such situations rather than encouraging the understandable tendency of the child to avoid them altogether.

**8. Teach the Child to Make Better Use
of His or Her Visual-Perceptual-Organizational Skills**

It should be borne in mind that children tend to "lead with their strong suit" in situations that are in any way problematic for them. For example, if a child exhibits an outstanding area of disability (e.g., visual-spatial skills) in combination with relatively intact abilities (e.g., verbal receptive and verbal expressive skills), he or she tends to use the better developed (verbal) skills whenever it is possible, even though inappropriate, to do so. This encourages a situation in which the poorly developed skills (e.g., visual-spatial skills) are not challenged or "exercised"; hence, optimal development may not be realized. The tendency to "play one's strong suit" also encourages the child with NLD to develop a very wide variety of ways to use language-related skills, many of which are clearly maladaptive.

To increase the likelihood that the child's visual modality and associated perceptive and analytic abilities will be developed and used optimally, a younger child of this type could be taught to name visual details in pictures as a way of encouraging him or her to pay attention to these details. In conjunction with this exercise, the child could be asked to talk about the relationship between various details in a picture (e.g., intersecting lines) as a way of drawing attention to the complexity, importance, and significance of visual features of stimulus presentation.

When the child is older, remedial suggestions and exercises should be more "functional" or practical in nature, but at the same time should address directly the child's outstanding areas of difficulty. For example, consider the fact that most social situations require the child to decipher or decode the nonverbal behaviors of others in order to interpret them properly. It is clear that the child with NLD is quite deficient in abilities that are crucial for the development of nonverbal social-analytic skills. Therefore, one might create "artificial" social situations that require the child to rely only on his or her visual-receptive and other nonverbal skills for interpretation. This could be done with pictures, films, or even contrived "real-life" situations for which there is no verbal feedback available. After an exercise of this type, one should discuss the child's perception of the social situation and of his or her most appropriate role in the situation. At the same time, one might provide the child with strategies for deciphering the most salient nonverbal dimensions inherent in these contrived social situations.

9. Teach the Child to Interpret Visual Information When There Is "Competing" Auditory Information

This type of training is usually more complex than the suggested remedial interventions already mentioned. This recommendation is particularly important when attempting to teach the child to deal more effectively with novel social situations. In these situations, it is important not only to interpret others' nonverbal behavior correctly, but also to interpret what is being said in conjunction with these nonverbal cues. In most cases, this type of training should be undertaken only when there has been adequate work and progress in the previously mentioned areas.

Example: Have the child observe videotaped interactions that contain varying degrees of complexity in terms of physical and psychological cause-effect relationships. Encourage the child to examine all of the information available before generating a "solution" to the problem and/or anticipating the next step in the action sequence. In this genre of activities, as in so many others, it is necessary to adopt ways and means to quell the child's rather predominant tendency to proceed without due concern for all—or even most—of the elements necessary to comprehend and deal effectively with complex or novel situations.

10. Teach Appropriate Nonverbal Behavior

Many children with NLD do not appear to have adequately developed nonverbal behavior. For example, such children often present with a somewhat "vacant look" or other inappropriate facial expressions. This is especially the case for those individuals who are found to exhibit marked neuropsychological deficits. The child with NLD may smile in situations in which such behavior is quite inappropriate (e.g., when he or she is experiencing failure with a task). It is important to attempt to teach more appropriate nonverbal behavior, keeping in mind the concepts introduced in association with the refinements of the child's verbal expressive skills. In this connection, teaching the child "what to do" and "how and when to do it" should be the focus of concern. For example, some children may not know how or when to convey their feelings in a nonverbal manner. The use of informative pictures, imitative "drills," work with a mirror, and other techniques and concrete aids can prove to be invaluable in this type of training. This sort of intervention may also serve to make the child more aware of the significance of the nonverbal behavior of others.

Example: Encourage the development of mime. Have the child confine his or her own communication to nonverbal means for certain periods during the day, and encourage the child to interpret the mimed communication of others on videotape or in real time interactions. Although the child with NLD finds this to be very difficult to countenance initially, staying with a regimen that involves regular periods of nonverbal communication (both sending and receiving) can be very effective in achieving worthwhile adaptive goals.

11. Facilitate Structured Peer Interactions

It is not always possible to promote social training in unstructured social situations, because these are largely beyond the reach of the remedial therapist or teacher. For instance, when the child is on the playground, it is not often possible to regulate his or her play in any way (at least to the extent that it promotes positive social growth for the socially impaired youngster). However, intramural activities of one sort or another, clubs, and formal community groups can provide a forum for social training if exploited in a proper manner. Unfortunately, because many children of this type tend to be somewhat socially withdrawn, they may not be encouraged to join their peers in social activities of any kind because their parents and other caregivers may see the need to protect the child from such encounters.

This raises the thorny issue of "overprotection." Although sensitive caregivers are often accused of this, it is clear that they may be the only ones who have an appreciation for the child's vulnerability and lack of appropriate skill development. Balancing the need for protection with the need for expanded horizons and encounters with physical and social reality is never easy. Understanding that this is a difficult realm within which to exercise prudence (i.e., to dare wisely) is the first—and very necessary—step to engaging in the complex series of judgments and activities that constitute the building blocks for effective intervention for children with NLD.

12. Promote, Encourage, and Monitor
"Systematic" Explorative Activities

One of the most potentially harmful tacks that a well-meaning therapist can take with the child with NLD is to leave the child to his or her own devices in activities that lack sufficient (or any) structure (e.g., ambient play situations with other children). On the other hand, it is quite worthwhile to design specific activities through which the child is encouraged to explore his or her environment. For example, exploratory activity may be encouraged within the structure of a gross motor program. In this setting, the child could be provided with the opportunity to explore various types of apparatus and the exercises that would suit each apparatus. In this situation, it is important that children do not feel that they are competing with their peers. In addition, following the lesson, the child should be required to give the instructor some verbal feedback and, perhaps, accompanying demonstrations regarding the activities that have transpired.

13. Teach the "Older" Child (at Least 10 Years of Age)
How to Use Available Aids to Reach a Specific Goal

One potential "aid" is a hand calculator, which could be used to provide the child with a way of checking the accuracy of his or her mechanical arithmetic work. After the child has completed a question independently, allow him or her to redo the same question with a hand calculator. This gives the child a means for checking the accuracy of the answer (as long as the hand calculator is used correctly). If it is found that the solution is incorrect, the child should then be encouraged to rework the question with pen and paper. At the high school level, hand calculators should probably be used whenever possible, so that the adolescent or young adult will develop at least a functional grasp of common mathematical operations and their applications in everyday life situations.

Another aid that could be used, especially for the younger child of this type, is a digital watch. We have found that many such children have difficulty in reading the hands of a traditional type of clock-face, and that this imposes further limitations on their already impoverished appreciation of time concepts. A digital watch is more easily read and can serve as a concrete tool for the teaching of elementary time concepts.

In all of this, there is no substitute for creative approaches to the provision of therapeutic "aids." This is especially the case for the exploitation of the vast potential of computers as prosthetic/therapeutic devices. Programs that allow for appropriate and helpful corrective feedback for difficult academic subjects, those that take the child in a step-by-step fashion through any number of quasi-social and problem-solving situations, those that present material in a systematic, sequenced fashion that draws the child's attention to the process of problem-solving development—all of these and many more dimensions of the creative use of computer software are potentially of considerable benefit for the child and adolescent with NLD.

14. Help the Child to Gain Insight
Into Situations That Are Easy for Him or Her
and Those That Are Potentially Troublesome

It is important for older children and adolescents with NLD to gain a reasonably realistic view of their capabilities. This is certainly more easily said than done. In this regard, the therapist's expectations always need to be in concert with the child's abilities, because gains in this area may prove to be marginal at best. For instance, it may be that the child's practical insight may be limited to "I am good at spelling and have problems with math." However, if the child is provided with consistent and appropriate feedback from concerned and informed adults regarding his or her performances in various kinds of situations, fairly sophisticated insights may develop. This is especially important with respect to perceiving the need for the utilization of prelearned strategies in appropriate situations. Furthermore, it is important that children with NLD learn that they do have some cognitive strengths and that these strengths can be used to advantage in specific situations.

15. Work With All of the Child's Caregivers
to Help Them With Insight and Direction
Regarding the Child's Most Salient Development Needs

All of the recommendations that have been made above can apply to the style and emphasis that all caregivers could incorporate in their relations with the child with NLD. We have found that well-motivated caregivers who have an intuitive or learned appreciation of such a child's adaptive strengths and weaknesses most often create a milieu at home or elsewhere in which the child prospers and in which adaptive deficits are minimized. Unfortunately this ideal caregiver-child relationship is not often found; in consequence, it is often necessary for the concerned professional to assume a major responsibility for guiding the child's principal caregivers. In some cases, it may be advisable and/or necessary to employ highly structured "parenting" programs (e.g., Directive Parental Counselling; Holland, 1983) to assist in the role of various caregivers in the habilitational process.

16. Other Recommendations

Among the other specific educational recommendations for this type of child are the following: (a) Teach and emphasize reading comprehension skills as soon as the child has gained a functional appreciation of sound-symbol correspondence; (b) institute regular drills early in the child's educational career to help further development of his or her handwriting skills; (c) before any copying task, teach the child to read carefully the material to be copied; (d) teach the child (verbal) strategies that will help him or her to organize written work; (e) teach mechanical arithmetic in a systematic, verbal, step-by-step fashion, as outlined in some detail elsewhere (see above and Strang & Rourke, 1985b); (f) involve the child as much as possible in skill-level appropriate physical education experiences. With respect to the latter point, it should be borne in mind that motor learning of all sorts is difficult, but necessary, for the child with NLD. Indeed, because such children learn to decode words and spell at superior levels without any appreciable teaching or other assistance, it would be well to substitute various types of "physical" activities during times when word decoding and spelling are being taught to his or her classmates.

17. Be Cognizant of the Therapist's/Remedial Specialist's Role in Preparing the Child With NLD for Adult Life

Special educators, in particular, should assume a major role in preparing this type of child for adult life. Unlike most educational programs, in which the primary goal is to help the child to master a particular curriculum, the program required by children with NLD is one that focuses primarily on the development of life skills. The child's mastery of the standard academic curriculum is insignificant if he or she is not prepared to meet the social and other adaptive demands of independent living. Indeed, we have found through longitudinal follow-up that some children with NLD as adults have developed rather seriously debilitating forms of psychopathology. This being the case, it is clear that remedial/habilitational interventions with such children should always be consonant with their short- and long-term remedial needs and remedial capacities.

REFERENCES

Achenbach, T. M., & Edelbrock, C. S. (1983). *Manual for the Child Behavior Checklist and Revised Child Behavior Profile.* Burlington: University of Vermont, Department of Psychiatry.

Ackerman, D., & Howes, C. (1986). Sociometric status and after-school activity of children with learning disabilities. *Journal of Learning Disabilities, 19,* 416-419.

Ansara, A., Geschwind, N., Galaburda, A., Albert, M., & Gartrell, N. (Eds.). (1981). *Sex differences in dyslexia.* Towson, MD: Orton Dyslexia Society.

Applebee, A. N. (1971). Research in reading retardation: Two critical problems. *Journal of Child Psychology and Psychiatry, 12,* 91-113.

Bakker, D. J. (1967). Temporal order, meaningfulness and reading ability. *Perceptual and Motor Skills, 24,* 1027-1030.

Bakker, D. J. (1986). Electrophysiological validation of L- and P-type dyslexia. *Journal of Clinical and Experimental Neuropsychology, 8,* 133.

Bakker, D. J. (1990). *Neuropsychological treatment of dyslexia.* New York: Oxford University Press.

Bakker, D. J., Licht, R., Kok, A., & Bouma, A. (1980). Cortical responses to word reading by right- and left-eared normal and reading-disturbed children. *Journal of Clinical and Experimental Neuropsychology, 2,* 1-12.

Bakker, D. J., Licht, R., & Van Strien, J. (1991). Biopsychological validation of L- and P-type dyslexia. In B. P. Rourke (Ed.), *Neuropsychological validation of learning disability subtypes* (pp. 124-139). New York: Guilford.

Barkley, R. A. (1990). *Attention deficit hyperactivity disorder: A handbook for diagnosis and treatment.* New York: Guilford.

Bender, W. N. (1987). Correlates of classroom behavior problems among learning disabled and nondisabled children in mainstream classes. *Learning Disabilities Quarterly, 10,* 317-324.

Benson, D. F., & Geschwind, N. (1970). Developmental Gerstmann syndrome. *Neurology, 20,* 293-298.

Benton, A. L. (1965). *Sentence memory test.* Iowa City, IA: Author.

Benton, A. L. (1975). Developmental dyslexia: Neurological aspects. In W. J. Friedlander (Ed.), *Advances in neurology* (Vol. 7, pp. 1-41). New York: Raven Press.

Brandys, C. F., & Rourke, B. P. (1991). Differential memory capacities in reading- and arithmetic-disabled children. In B. P. Rourke (Ed.), *Neuropsychological validation of learning disability subtypes* (pp. 73-96). New York: Guilford.

Brown, S. J., Rourke, B. P., & Cicchetti, D. V. (1989). Reliability of tests and measures used in the neuropsychological assessment of children. *The Clinical Neuropsychologist, 3,* 353-368.

Brumback, R. A., & Staton, R. D. (1983). Learning disabilities and childhood depression. *American Journal of Orthopsychiatry, 53,* 269-281.

Buschke, H. (1974). Components of verbal learning in children: Analysis by selective reminding. *Journal of Experimental Child Psychology, 18,* 488-496.

Casey, J. E., Del Dotto, J. E., & Rourke, B. P. (1990). An empirical investigation of the NLD syndrome in a case of agenesis of the corpus callosum. *Journal of Clinical and Experimental Neuropsychology, 12,* 29.

Casey, J. E., Rourke, B. R., & Picard, E. (1991). Syndrome of Nonverbal Learning Disabilities: Age differences in neuropsychological, academic, and socioemotional functioning. *Development and Psychopathology, 3,* 329-345.

CELDIC Report. (1970). *One million children: A national study of Canadian children with emotional and learning disorders.* Toronto: Leonard Crainford.

Cermak, S. A., & Murray, E. (1992). Nonverbal learning disabilities in the adult framed in the model of human occupation. In N. Katz (Ed.), *Cognitive rehabilitation: Models for intervention in occupational therapy* (pp. 258-291). Boston: Andover Medical.

Chapman, J. W. (1988). Cognitive-motivational characteristics and academic achievement of learning disabled children: A longitudinal study. *Journal of Educational Psychology, 80,* 357-365.

Chapman, J. W., & Boersma, F. J. (1980). *Affective correlates of learning disabilities.* Lisse, The Netherlands: Swets & Zeitlinger.

Colbert, P., Newman, B., Ney, P., & Young, J. (1982). Learning disabilities as a symptom of depression in children. *Journal of Learning Disabilities, 15,* 333-336.

Cook, T. D., & Campbell, D. T. (1979). *Quasi-experimentation: Design and analysis issues for field settings.* Boston: Houghton Mifflin.

Czudner, G., & Rourke, B. P. (1972). Age differences in visual reaction time in "brain-damaged" and normal children under regular and irregular preparatory interval conditions. *Journal of Experimental Child Psychology, 13,* 516-526.

DeFries, J. C., Fulker, D. W., & LaBuda, M. C. (1987). Evidence for a genetic aetiology in reading disability of twins. *Nature, 329,* 537-539.

Del Dotto, J. E., Fisk, J. L., McFadden, G. T., & Rourke, B. P. (1991). Developmental analysis of children/adolescents with nonverbal learning disabilities: Long-term impact on personality adjustment and patterns of adaptive functioning. In B. P. Rourke (Ed.), *Neuropsychological validation of learning disability subtypes* (pp. 293-308). New York: Guilford.

Del Dotto, J. E., Rourke, B. P., McFadden, G. T., & Fisk, J. L. (1987). Developmental analysis of arithmetic-disabled children: Impact on personality adjustment and patterns of adaptive functioning. *Journal of Clinical and Experimental Neuropsychology, 9,* 44.

DeLuca, J. W., Rourke, B. P., & Del Dotto, J. E. (1991). Subtypes of arithmetic-disabled children: Cognitive and personality dimensions. In B. P. Rourke (Ed.), *Neuropsychological validation of learning disability subtypes* (pp. 180-219). New York: Guilford.

Dixon, R., & Engelmann, S. (1979). *Corrective spelling through morphographs.* Chicago: Science Research Associates.

Doehring, D. G. (1968). *Patterns of impairment in specific reading disability*. Bloomington: Indiana University Press.

Doehring, D. G. (1978). The tangled web of behavioral research on developmental dyslexia. In A. L. Benton & D. Pearl (Eds.), *Dyslexia: An appraisal of current knowledge* (pp. 125-135). New York: Oxford University Press.

Doehring, D. G., & Hoschko, I. M. (1977). Classification of reading problems by the Q-technique of factor analysis. *Cortex, 13*, 281-294.

Doehring, D. G., Hoschko, I. M., & Bryans, B. N. (1979). Statistical classification of children with reading problems. *Journal of Clinical Neuropsychology, 1*, 5-16.

Dool, C. B., Stelmack, R. M., & Rourke, B. P. (1993). Event-related potentials in children with learning disabilities. *Journal of Clinical Child Psychology, 22*, 387-398.

Dunn, L. M. (1965). *Expanded manual for the Peabody Picture Vocabulary Test*. Minneapolis, MN: American Guidance Service.

Dunn, L. M., & Markwardt, F. C. (1970). *Manual for the Peabody Individual Achievement Test*. Circle Pines, MN: American Guidance Service.

Edelbrock, C. S., & Achenbach, T. M. (1984). The teacher version of the Child Behavior Profile: I. Boys aged 6-11. *Journal of Consulting and Clinical Psychology, 52*, 207-217.

Ehrlich, M. I. (1983). Psychofamilial correlates of school disorders. *Journal of School Psychology, 21*, 191-199.

Everitt, B. (1980). *Cluster analysis*. New York: Halsted Press.

Fiedorowicz, C. A. M., & Trites, R. L. (1991). From theory to practice with subtypes of reading disabilities. In B. P. Rourke (Ed.), *Neuropsychological validation of learning disability subtypes* (pp. 243-266). New York: Guilford.

Fisk, J. L., & Rourke, B. P. (1979). Identification of subtypes of learning-disabled children at three age levels: A neuropsychological, multivariate approach. *Journal of Clinical Neuropsychology, 1*, 289-310.

Fletcher, J. M. (1985). External validation of learning disability typologies. In B. P. Rourke (Ed.), *Neuropsychology of learning disabilities: Essentials of subtype analysis* (pp. 187-211). New York: Guilford.

Fletcher, J. M., Bohan, T. P., Brandt, M. E., Brookshire, B. L., Beaver, S. R., Francis, D. J., Davidson, K. C., Thompson, N. M., & Miner, M. E. (1992). Cerebral white matter and cognition in hydrocephalic children. *Archives of Neurology, 49*, 818-825.

Fletcher, J. M., & Copeland, D. R. (1988). Neurobehavioral effects of central nervous system prophylactic treatment of cancer in children. *Journal of Clinical and Experimental Neuropsychology, 10*, 495-537.

Fletcher, J. M., Francis, D. J., Thompson, N. M., Brookshire, B. L., Bohan, T. P., Landry, S. H., Davidson, K. C., & Miner, M. E. (1992). Verbal and nonverbal skill discrepancies in hydrocephalic children. *Journal of Clinical and Experimental Neuropsychology, 14*, 593-609.

Fletcher, J. M., & Levin, H. (1988). Neurobehavioral effects of brain injury in children. In D. K. Routh (Ed.), *Handbook of pediatric psychology* (pp. 258-295). New York: Guilford.

Fletcher, J. M., & Satz, P. (1980). Developmental changes in the neuropsychological correlates of reading achievement: A six-year longitudinal follow-up. *Journal of Clinical Neuropsychology, 2*, 23-37.

Fletcher, J. M., & Satz, P. (1985). Cluster analysis and the search for learning disability subtypes. In B. P. Rourke (Ed.), *Neuropsychology of learning disabilities: Essentials of subtype analysis* (pp. 40-64). New York: Guilford.

Fletcher, J. M., & Taylor, H. G. (1984). Neuropsychological approaches to children: Towards a developmental neuropsychology. *Journal of Clinical Neuropsychology, 6,* 39-56.

Francis, D. J., Fletcher, J. M., & Rourke, B. P. (1988). Discriminant validity of lateral sensorimotor measures in children. *Journal of Clinical and Experimental Neuropsychology, 10,* 779-799.

Francis, D. J., Fletcher, J. M., Rourke, B. P., & York, M. J. (1992). A five-factor model for motor, psychomotor, and visual-spatial tests in the neuropsychological assessment of children. *Journal of Clinical and Experimental Neuropsychology, 14,* 625-637.

Fuerst, D. R., Fisk, J. L., & Rourke, B. P. (1989). Psychosocial functioning of learning-disabled children: Replicability of statistically derived subtypes. *Journal of Consulting and Clinical Psychology, 57,* 275-280.

Fuerst, D. R., Fisk, J. L., & Rourke, B. P. (1990). Psychosocial functioning of learning-disabled children: Relations between WISC Verbal IQ-Performance IQ discrepancies and personality subtypes. *Journal of Consulting and Clinical Psychology, 58,* 657-660.

Fuerst, D. R., & Rourke, B. P. (1993). Psychosocial functioning of children: Relations between personality subtypes and academic achievement. *Journal of Abnormal Child Psychology, 21,* 597-607.

Fuerst, D. R., & Rourke, B. P. (1993). Patterns of psychosocial functioning of children with learning disabilities at three age levels. (Manuscript under review)

Galante, M. B., Flye, M. E., & Stephens, L. S. (1972). Cumulative minor deficits: A longitudinal study of the relation of physical factors to school achievement. *Journal of Learning Disabilities, 5,* 75-80.

Glosser, G., & Koppell, S. (1987). Emotional-behavioral patterns in children with LD: Lateralized hemispheric differences. *Journal of Learning Disabilities, 20,* 365-368.

Golding-Kushner, K. J., Weller, G., & Shprintzen, R. J. (1985). Velo-cardio-facial syndrome: Language and psychological profiles. *Journal of Craniofacial Genetics and Developmental Biology, 5,* 259-266.

Goyette, C. H., Connors, C. K., & Ulrich, R. F. (1978). Normative data on Revised Connors Parent and Teacher Rating Scales. *Journal of Abnormal Child Psychology, 6,* 221-236.

Green, K. D., Forehand, R., Beck, S. J., & Vosk, B. (1980). An assessment of the relationship among measures of children's social competence, and children's academic achievement. *Child Development, 51,* 1149-1156.

Grunau, R. V. E., & Low, M. D. (1987). Cognitive and task-related EEG correlates of arithmetic performance in adolescents. *Journal of Clinical and Experimental Neuropsychology, 9,* 563-574.

Hallgren, B. (1950). Specific dyslexia ("congenital word blindness"): A clinical and genetic study. *ACTA Psychiatrica et Neurologica Scandinavica,* Suppl. No. 65.

Harnadek, M. C. S., & Rourke, B. P. (1994). Principal identifying features of the syndrome of nonverbal learning disabilities in children. *Journal of Learning Disabilities, 27,* 144-154.

Hermann, K. (1959). *Reading disability: A medical study of word blindness and related handicaps.* Copenhagen: Munksgaard.

Holland, C. J. (1983). *Directive parental counseling: The counselor's guide.* Bloomfield Hills, MI: Midwest Professional Publishing.

Jastak, J. F., & Jastak, S. R. (1965). *The Wide Range Achievement Test.* Wilmington, DE: Guidance Associates.

Jastak, S. R., & Wilkinson, G. S. (1984). *The Wide Range Achievement Test.* Wilmington, DE: Guidance Associates.

Johnson, D. J., & Myklebust, H. R. (1967). *Learning disabilities.* New York: Grune & Stratton.

Jorm, A. F., Share, D. L., Matthews, R., & Maclean, R. (1986). Behavior problems in specific reading retarded and general reading backward children: A longitudinal study. *Journal of Child Psychology and Psychiatry, 27,* 33-43.

Joschko, M., & Rourke, B. P. (1985). Neuropsychological subtypes of learning-disabled children who exhibit the ACID pattern on the WISC. In B. P. Rourke (Ed.), *Neuropsychology of learning disabilities: Essentials of subtype analysis* (pp. 65-88). New York: Guilford.

Kass, C. E. (1964). Auditory Closure Test. In J. J. Olson & J. L. Olson (Eds.), *Validity studies on the Illinois Test of Psycholinguistic Abilities.* Madison, WI: Photo.

Kawi, A. A., & Pasamanick, B. (1959). Prenatal and perinatal factors in the development of child reading disorders. *Monographs of the Society for Research in Child Development, 24.*

Kinsbourne, M., & Warrington, E. K. (1963). The developmental Gerstmann syndrome. *Archives of Neurology, 8,* 490-501.

Kirk, S. A., & McCarthy, J. J. (1961). The Illinois Test of Psycholinguistic Abilities: An approach to differential diagnosis. *American Journal of Mental Deficiency, 66,* 399-412.

Klove, H. (1963). Clinical neuropsychology. In F. M. Forster (Ed.), *The medical clinics of North America* (pp. 1647-1658). New York: W. B. Saunders.

Knights, R. M., & Norwood, J. A. (1980). *Revised smoothed normative data on the neuropsychological test battery for children.* Ottawa: Author.

Korhonen, T. T. (1991). An empirical subgrouping of Finnish learning-disabled children. *Journal of Clinical and Experimental Neuropsychology, 13,* 259-277.

Laslo, J. I., & Broderick, P. (1991). Drawing and handwriting difficulties: Reasons for and remediation of dysfunction. In J. Wann, A. M. Wing, & N. Sovik (Eds.), *Development of graphic skills: Research perspectives and educational implications* (pp. 259-280). New York: Academic Press.

Levine, M. D., Oberklaid, F., & Meltzer, L. (1981). Developmental output failure: A study of low productivity in school-aged children. *Pediatrics, 67,* 18-25.

Loveland, K. A., Fletcher, J. M., & Bailey, V. (1990). Nonverbal communication of events in learning-disability subtypes. *Journal of Clinical and Experimental Neuropsychology, 12,* 433-447.

Lovrich, D., & Stamm, J. S. (1983). Event-related potential and behavioral correlates of attention in reading retardation. *Journal of Clinical and Experimental Neuropsychology, 5,* 13-37.

Lyon, G. R. (1985). Educational validation studies of learning disability subtypes. In B. P. Rourke (Ed.), *Neuropsychology of learning disabilities: Essentials of subtype analysis* (pp. 257-280). New York: Guilford.

Lyon, G. R., & Flynn, J. M. (1991). Educational validation studies with subtypes of learning-disabled readers. In B. P. Rourke (Ed.), *Neuropsychological validation of learning disability subtypes* (pp. 223-242). New York: Guilford.

Mattis, S., French, J. H., & Rapin, I. (1975). Dyslexia in children and young adults: Three independent neuropsychological syndromes. *Developmental Medicine and Child Neurology, 17,* 150-163.

Mattson, A. J., Sheer, D. E., & Fletcher, J. M. (1992). Electrophysiological evidence of lateralized disturbances in children with learning disabilities. *Journal of Clinical and Experimental Neuropsychology, 14,* 718-727.

McConaughy, S. H., & Ritter, D. R. (1986). Social competence and behavioral problems of learning disabled boys aged 6-11. *Journal of Learning Disabilities, 19,* 39-45.

McCue, M., & Goldstein, G. (1991). Neuropsychological aspects of learning disability in adults. In B. P. Rourke (Ed.), *Neuropsychological validation of learning disability subtypes* (pp. 311-329). New York: Guilford.

McKinney, J. D., Short, E. J., & Feagans, L. (1985). Academic consequences of perceptual-linguistic subtypes of learning-disabled children. *Learning Disabilities Research, 1,* 6-17.

McKinney, J. D., & Speece, D. L. (1986). Academic consequences and longitudinal stability of behavioral subtypes of learning disabled children. *Journal of Educational Psychology, 78,* 365-372.

Miles, J. E., & Stelmack, R. M. (in press). Reading disability subtypes and the effects of auditory and visual priming on event-related potentials. *Journal of Clinical and Experimental Neuropsychology.*

Morris, R., Blashfield, R., & Satz, P. (1981). Neuropsychology and cluster analysis: Potentials and problems. *Journal of Clinical Neuropsychology, 3,* 79-99.

Morris, R., Blashfield, R., & Satz, P. (1986). Developmental classification of reading-disabled children. *Journal of Clinical and Experimental Neuropsychology, 8,* 371-392.

Morris, R. D., & Fletcher, J. M. (1988). Classification in neuropsychology: A theoretical framework and research paradigm. *Journal of Clinical and Experimental Neuropsychology, 10,* 640-658.

Morris, R. D., & Walter, L. W. (1991). Subtypes of arithmetic-disabled adults: Validating childhood findings. In B. P. Rourke (Ed.), *Neuropsychological validation of learning disability subtypes* (pp. 330-346). New York: Guilford.

Nass, R., Speiser, P., Heier, L., Haimes, A., & New, M. (1990). White matter abnormalities in congenital adrenal hyperplasia. *Annals of Neurology, 28,* 470.

Nussbaum, N. L., & Bigler, E. D. (1986). Neuropsychological and behavioral profiles of empirically derived subgroups of learning disabled children. *International Journal of Clinical Neuropsychology, 8,* 82-89.

Nussbaum, N. L., Bigler, E. D., Koch, W. R., Ingram, W., Rosa, L., & Massman, P. (1988). Personality/behavioral characteristics in children: Differential effects of putative anterior versus posterior cerebral asymmetry. *Archives of Clinical Neuropsychology, 3,* 127-135.

Owen, F. W. (1978). Dyslexia: Genetic aspects. In A. L. Benton & D. Pearl (Eds.), *Dyslexia: An appraisal of current knowledge* (pp. 267-284). New York: Oxford University Press.

Ozols, E. J., & Rourke, B. P. (1985). Dimensions of social sensitivity in two types of learning-disabled children. In B. P. Rourke (Ed.), *Neuropsychology of learning disabilities: Essentials of subtype analysis* (pp. 281-301). New York: Guilford.

Ozols, E. J., & Rourke, B. P. (1988). Characteristics of young learning-disabled children classified according to patterns of academic achievement: Auditory-perceptual and visual-perceptual disabilities. *Journal of Clinical Child Psychology, 17,* 44-52.

Ozols, E. J., & Rourke, B. P. (1991). Classification of young learning-disabled children according to patterns of academic achievement: Validity studies. In B. P. Rourke (Ed.), *Neuropsychological validation of learning disability subtypes* (pp. 97-123). New York: Guilford.

Petrauskas, R. J., & Rourke, B. P. (1979). Identification of subtypes of retarded readers: A neuropsychological, multivariate approach. *Journal of Clinical Neuropsychology, 1,* 17-37.

Piaget, J. (1954). *The construction of reality in the child*. New York: Basic Books.

Porter, J., E., & Rourke, B. P. (1985). Personality and socioemotional dimensions of learning disabilities in children. In B. P. Rourke (Ed.), *Neuropsychology of learning disabilities: Essentials of subtype analysis* (pp. 257-280). New York: Guilford.

Reitan, R. M. (1966). A research program on the psychological effects of brain lesions in human beings. In N. R. Ellis (Ed.), *International review of research in mental retardation, Vol. 1*. (pp. 153-218). New York: Academic Press.

Reitan, R. M. (1974). Methodological problems in clinical neuropsychology. In R. M. Reitan & L. A. Davison (Eds.), *Clinical neuropsychology: Current status and applications* (pp. 19-46). New York: John Wiley.

Reitan, R. M., & Davison, L. A. (Eds.). (1974). *Clinical neuropsychology: Current status and applications*. New York: John Wiley.

Reports of the INS-Division 40 Task Force on Education, Accreditation, and Credentialing. (1987). *The Clinical Neuropsychologist, 1*, 29-34.

Rosner, J., & Simon, D. P. (1970). *Auditory Analysis Test: An initial report*. Pittsburgh: Author. [Available from Learning Research and Development Center, University of Pittsburgh]

Rourke, B. P. (1975). Brain-behavior relationships in children with learning disabilities. *American Psychologist, 30*, 911-920.

Rourke, B. P. (1976a). Issues in the neuropsychological assessment of children with learning disabilities. *Canadian Psychological Review, 17*, 89-102.

Rourke, B. P. (1976b). Reading retardation in children: Developmental lag or deficit? In R. M. Knights & D. J. Bakker (Eds.), *Neuropsychology of learning disorders: Theoretical approaches* (pp. 125-137). Baltimore: University Park Press.

Rourke, B. P. (1978a). Neuropsychological research in reading retardation: A review. In A. L. Benton & D. Pearl (Eds.), *Dyslexia: An appraisal of current knowledge* (pp. 141-171). New York: Oxford University Press.

Rourke, B. P. (1978b). Reading, spelling, arithmetic disabilities: A neuropsychologic perspective. In H. R. Myklebust (Ed.), *Progress in learning disabilities* (Vol. 4, pp. 97-120). New York: Grune & Stratton.

Rourke, B. P. (1981). Neuropsychological assessment of children with learning disabilities. In S. B. Filskov & T. J. Boll (Eds.), *Handbook of clinical neuropsychology* (pp. 453-478). New York: John Wiley.

Rourke, B. P. (1982). Central processing deficiencies in children: Toward a developmental neuropsychological model. *Journal of Clinical Neuropsychology, 4*, 1-18.

Rourke, B. P. (1983). Reading and spelling disabilities: A developmental neuropsychological perspective. In U. Kirk (Ed.), *Neuropsychology of language, reading, and spelling* (pp. 209-234). New York: Academic Press.

Rourke, B. P. (Ed.). (1985). *Neuropsychology of learning disabilities: Essentials of subtype analysis*. New York: Guilford.

Rourke, B. P. (1987). Syndrome of nonverbal learning disabilities: The final common pathway of white-matter disease/dysfunction? *The Clinical Neuropsychologist, 1*, 209-234.

Rourke, B. P. (1988a). Socioemotional disturbances of learning-disabled children. *Journal of Consulting and Clinical Psychology, 56*, 801-810.

Rourke, B. P. (1988b). The syndrome of nonverbal learning disabilities: Developmental manifestations in neurological disease, disorder, and dysfunction. *The Clinical Neuropsychologist, 2*, 293-330.

Rourke, B. P. (1989). *Nonverbal learning disabilities: The syndrome and the model.* New York: Guilford.

Rourke, B. P. (1991). *Neuropsychological validation of learning disability subtypes.* New York: Guilford.

Rourke, B. P. (1993). Arithmetic disabilities, specific and otherwise: A neuropsychological perspective. *Journal of Learning Disabilities, 26,* 214-226.

Rourke, B. P., Bakker, D. J., Fisk, J. L., & Strang, J. D. (1983). *Child neuropsychology: An introduction to theory, research, and clinical practice.* New York: Guilford.

Rourke, B. P., & Czudner, G. (1972). Age differences in auditory reaction time in "brain-damaged" and normal children under regular and irregular preparatory interval conditions. *Journal of Experimental Child Psychology, 14,* 372-378.

Rourke, B. P., & Del Dotto, J. E. (1992). Learning disabilities: A neuropsychological perspective. In C. E. Walker & M. C. Roberts (Eds.), *Handbook of clinical child psychology* (2nd ed.) (pp. 511-536). New York: John Wiley.

Rourke, B. P., Del Dotto, J. E., Rourke, S. B., & Casey, J. E. (1990). Nonverbal learning disabilities: The syndrome and a case study. *Journal of School Psychology, 28,* 361-385.

Rourke, B. P., Dietrich, D. M., & Young, G. C. (1973). Significance of WISC verbal-performance discrepancies for younger children with learning disabilities. *Perceptual and Motor Skills, 36,* 275-282.

Rourke, B. P., & Finlayson, M. A. J. (1978). Neuropsychological significance of variations in patterns of academic performance: Verbal and visual abilities. *Journal of Abnormal Child Psychology, 6,* 121-133.

Rourke, B. P., & Fisk, J. L. (1976). *Children's Word-Finding Test (Revised).* Windsor, Ontario: Author. [Available from Department of Psychology, University of Windsor, Windsor, Ontario, Canada]

Rourke, B. P., & Fisk, J. L. (1981). Socio-emotional disturbances of learning-disabled children: The role of central processing deficits. *Bulletin of the Orton Society, 31,* 77-88.

Rourke, B. P., & Fisk, J. L. (1992). Adult presentations of learning disabilities. In R. F. White (Ed.), *Clinical syndromes in adult neuropsychology: The practitioner's handbook* (pp. 451-473). Amsterdam: Elsevier.

Rourke, B. P., Fisk, J. L., & Strang, J. D. (1986). *Neuropsychological assessment of children: A treatment-oriented approach.* New York: Guilford.

Rourke, B. P., & Fuerst, D. R. (1991). *Learning disabilities and psychosocial functioning: A neuropsychological perspective.* New York: Guilford.

Rourke, B. P., & Gates, R. D. (1980). *Underlining Test: Preliminary norms.* Windsor, Ontario: Author. [Available from Department of Psychology, University of Windsor, Windsor, Ontario, Canada]

Rourke, B. P., & Gates, R. D. (1981). Neuropsychological research and school psychology. In G. W. Hynd & J. E. Obrzut (Eds.), *Neuropsychological assessment and the school-age child: Issues and procedures* (pp. 3-25). New York: Grune & Stratton.

Rourke, B. P., & Petrauskas, R. J. (1977). *Underlining Test (Revised).* Windsor, Ontario: Author. [Available from Department of Psychology, University of Windsor, Windsor, Ontario, Canada]

Rourke, B. P., & Petrauskas, R. J. (1978). *Underlining Test* (Revised). Windsor, Ontario: Author. [Available from Department of Psychology, University of Windsor, Windsor, Ontario, Canada]

Rourke, B. P., & Strang, J. D. (1978). Neuropsychological significance of variations in patterns of academic performance: Motor, psychomotor, and tactile-perceptual abilities. *Journal of Pediatric Psychology, 3,* 62-66.

Rourke, B. P., & Strang, J. D. (1983). Subtypes of reading and arithmetical disabilities: A neuropsychological analysis. In M. Rutter (Ed.), *Developmental neuropsychiatry* (pp. 473-488). New York: Guilford.

Rourke, B. P., & Telegdy, G. A. (1971). Lateralizing significance of WISC verbal-performance discrepancies for older children with learning disabilities. *Perceptual and Motor Skills, 33,* 875-883.

Rourke, B. P., Young, G. C., & Flewelling, R. W. (1971). The relationships between WISC verbal-performance discrepancies and selected verbal, auditory-perceptual, visual-perceptual, and problem-solving abilities in children with learning disabilities. *Journal of Clinical Psychology, 27,* 475-479.

Rourke, B. P., Young, G. C., & Leenaars, A. (1989). A childhood learning disability that predisposes those afflicted to adolescent and adult depression and suicide risk. *Journal of Learning Disabilities, 21,* 169-175.

Rourke, B. P., Young, G. C., Strang, J. D., & Russell, D. L. (1986). Adult outcomes of central processing deficiencies in childhood. In I. Grant & K. M. Adams (Eds.), *Neuropsychological assessment in neuropsychiatric disorders: Clinical methods and empirical findings* (pp. 244-267). New York: Oxford University Press.

Rovet, J. F. (1989, June). *Effects of diabetes on neuropsychological functioning in children: A three-year prospective study.* Paper presented at the symposium, Neuropsychological Sequelae of Diabetes Mellitus, held at the meeting of the American Diabetes Association, Detroit.

Rovet, J. F. (1990). The cognitive and neuropsychological characteristics of females with Turner syndrome. In D. B. Berch & B. G. Berger (Eds.), *Sex chromosome abnormalities and human behavior* (pp. 38-77). Boulder, CO: Westview.

Rovet, J. F. (1993). The psychoeducational characteristics of children with Turner syndrome. *Journal of Learning Disabilities, 26,* 333-341.

Rovet, J. F., Ehrlich, R. M., Czuchta, D., & Akler, M. (in press). Psychoeducational characteristics of children and adolescents with insulin dependent diabetes mellitus. *Journal of Learning Disabilities, 26,* 7-22.

Rovet, J. F., & Netley, C. (1982). Processing deficits in Turner's syndrome. *Developmental Psychology, 18,* 77-94.

Shapiro, E. G., Lipton, M. E., & Krivit, W. (1992). White matter dysfunction and its neuropsychological correlates: A longitudinal study of a case of metachromatic leukodystrophy. *Journal of Clinical and Experimental Neuropsychology, 14,* 610-624.

Share, D. L., Moffitt, T. E., & Silva, P. A. (1988). Factors associated with arithmetic and reading disability and specific arithmetic disability. *Journal of Learning Disabilities, 21,* 313-320.

Siegel, L. S., & Feldman, W. (1982). Nondyslexic children with combined writing and arithmetic learning disabilities. *Clinical Pediatrics, 22,* 241-244.

Siegel, L. S., & Heaven, R. K. (1986). Categorization of learning disabilities. In S. J. Ceci (Ed.), *Handbook of cognitive, social, and neuropsychological aspects of learning disabilities* (Vol. 1, pp. 95-121). Hillsdale, NJ: Lawrence Erlbaum.

Silver, D. S., & Young, R. D. (1985). Interpersonal problem-solving abilities, peer status, and behavioral adjustment in learning disabled and non-learning disabled adolescents. *Advances in Learning and Behavioral Disabilities, 4,* 201-223.

Singer, J. E., Westphal, M., & Niswander, K. R. (1968). Sex differences in the incidence of neonatal abnormalities and abnormal performance of early childhood. *Child Development, 39,* 103.

Smith, S. D., Goldgar, D. E., Pennington, B. F., Kimberling, W. J., & Lubs, H. A. (1986). Analysis of subtypes of specific reading disability: Genetic and cluster analytic approaches. In G. Th. Pavlidis & D. F. Risher (Eds.), *Dyslexia: Its neuropsychology and treatment* (pp. 181-202). Chichester, UK: John Wiley.

Sparrow, S. S., Balla, D. A., & Cicchetti, D. V. (1984). *The Vineland Adaptive Behavior Scales: A revision of the Vineland Social Maturity Scale by Edgar A. Doll.* Circle Pines, MN: American Guidance Services.

Speece, D. L., McKinney, J. D., & Apelbaum, M. I. (1985). Classification and validation of behavioral subtypes of learning-disabled children. *Journal of Educational Psychology, 77,* 67-77.

Spreen, O. (1988). *Learning disabled children growing up: A follow-up into adulthood.* New York: Oxford University Press.

Spreen, O. (1989). The relationship between learning disabilities, emotional disorders, and neuropsychology: Some results and observations. *Journal of Clinical and Experimental Neuropsychology, 11,* 117-140.

Stellern, J., Marlowe, M., Jacobs, J., & Cossairt, A. (1985). Neuropsychological significance of right hemisphere cognitive mode in behavior disorders. *Behavioral Disorders, 2,* 113-124.

Stelmack, R. M., & Miles, J. (1990). The effect of picture priming on event-related potentials of normal and disabled readers during a word recognition memory task. *Journal of Clinical and Experimental Neuropsychology, 12,* 887-903.

Stevens, D. E., & Moffitt, T. E. (1988). Neuropsychological profile of an Asperger's syndrome case with exceptional calculating ability. *The Clinical Neuropsychologist, 2,* 228-238.

Strang, J. D. (1981). *Personality dimensions of learning disabled children: Age and subtype differences.* Unpublished doctoral dissertation, University of Windsor, Windsor, Ontario, Canada.

Strang, J. D., & Rourke, B. P. (1983). Concept-formation/non-verbal reasoning abilities of children who exhibit specific academic problems with arithmetic. *Journal of Clinical Child Psychology, 12,* 33-39.

Strang, J. D., & Rourke, B. P. (1985a). Adaptive behavior of children with specific arithmetic disabilities and associated neuropsychological abilities and deficits. In B. P. Rourke, (Ed.), *Neuropsychology of learning disabilities: Essentials of subtype analysis* (pp. 302-328). New York: Guilford.

Strang, J. D., & Rourke, B. P. (1985b). Arithmetic disability subtypes: The neuropsychological significance of specific arithmetical impairment in childhood. In B. P. Rourke (Ed.), *Neuropsychology of learning disabilities: Essentials of subtype analysis* (pp. 167-183). New York: Guilford.

Streissguth, A. P., & LaDue, R. A. (1987). Fetal alcohol syndrome: Teratogenic causes of developmental disabilities. In S. R. Schroeder (Ed.), *Toxic substances and mental retardation: Neurobehavioral toxicology and teratology* (pp. 1-32). Washington, DC: American Association on Mental Deficiency.

Sweeney, J. E., & Rourke, B. P. (1978). Neuropsychological significance of phonetically accurate and phonetically inaccurate spelling errors in younger and older retarded spellers. *Brain and Language, 5,* 212-225.

Szatmari, P., Tuff, L., Finlayson, M. A. J., & Bartolucci, G. (1990). Asperger's syndrome and autism: Neurocognitive aspects. *Journal of the American Academy of Child and Adolescent Psychiatry, 29,* 130-136.

Taylor, H. G. (1983). MBD: Meanings and misconceptions. *Journal of Clinical Neuropsychology, 5,* 271-287.

Taylor, H. G. (1989). Learning disabilities. In E. J. Mash & R. A. Barkley (Eds.), *Behavioral treatment of childhood disorders* (pp. 347-380). New York: Guilford.

Taylor, H. G., & Fletcher, J. M. (1983). Biological foundations of specific developmental disorders: Methods, findings, and future directions. *Journal of Clinical Child Psychology, 12,* 46-65.

Udwin, O., & Yule, W. (1988). *Infantile hypercalcaemia and Williams syndrome: Guidelines for parents.* Essex, UK: Infantile Hypercalcaemia Foundation.

Udwin, O., & Yule, W. (1989). *Infantile hypercalcaemia and Williams syndrome: Guidelines for teachers.* Essex, UK: Infantile Hypercalcaemia Foundation.

Udwin, O., & Yule, W. (1991). A cognitive and behavioural phenotype in Williams syndrome. *Journal of Clinical and Experimental Neuropsychology, 13,* 232-244.

van der Vlugt, H. (1991). Neuropsychological validation studies of learning disability subtypes: Verbal, visual-spatial, and psychomotor abilities. In B. P. Rourke (Ed.), *Neuropsychological validation of learning disability subtypes* (pp. 140-159). New York: Guilford.

van der Vlugt, H., & Satz, P. (1985). Subgroups and subtypes of learning-disabled and normal children: A cross-cultural replication. In B. P. Rourke (Ed.), *Neuropsychology of learning disabilities: Essentials of subtype analysis* (pp. 212-227). New York: Guilford.

Vaughn, S., Zaragoza, N., Hogan, A., & Walker, J. (1993). A four-year longitudinal investigation of the social skills and behavior problems of students with learning disabilities. *Journal of Learning Disabilities, 26,* 404-412.

Wechsler, D. (1949). *Wechsler Intelligence Scale for Children.* New York: Psychological Corporation.

Wechsler, D. (1974). *Wechsler Intelligence Scale for Children-Revised.* New York: Psychological Corporation.

Weller, C., & Strawser, S. (1987). Adaptive behavior of subtypes of learning disabled individuals. *Journal of Special Education, 21,* 101-115.

White, J. L., Moffitt, T. E., & Silva, P. A. (1992). Neuropsychological and socio-emotional correlates of specific-arithmetic disability. *Archives of Clinical Neuropsychology, 7,* 1-16.

Wiener, J. (1980). A theoretical model of the acquisition of peer relationships of learning disabled children. *Journal of Learning Disabilities, 13,* 42-47.

Williams, J. K., Richman, L., & Yarbrough, D. (1992). Comparison of visual spatial performance strategy training in children with Turner syndrome and learning disabilities. *Journal of Learning Disabilities, 25,* 658-664.

Wills, K. E., Holmbeck, G. N., Dillon, K., & McLone, D. G. (1990). Intelligence and achievement in children with myelomeningocele. *Journal of Pediatric Psychology, 15,* 161-176.

Wirt, R. D., Lachar, D., Klinedinst, J. K., & Seat, P. D. (1977). *Multidimensional description of child personality: A manual for the Personality Inventory for Children.* Los Angeles: Western Psychological Services.

Wirt, R. D., Lachar, D., Klinedinst, J. K., & Seat, P. D. (1984). *Multidimensional description of child personality: A manual for the Personality Inventory for Children, Revised 1984.* Los Angeles: Western Psychological Services.

INDEX

ABOUT THE AUTHORS

Byron P. Rourke, Ph.D., is Professor of Psychology and University Professor at the University of Windsor. He is also a member of the faculty of the Child Study Center, Yale University. He is Past President of the International Neuropsychological Society and of the Division of Clinical Neuropsychology of the American Psychological Association, and is currently President of the American Board of Clinical Neuropsychology. He is cofounder and coeditor of three journals: *Journal of Clinical and Experimental Neuropsychology; The Clinical Neuropsychologist;* and *Child Neuropsychology.* His authored and edited books include *Child Neuropsychology: An Introduction to Theory, Research, and Clinical Practice; Neuropsychology of Learning Disabilities: Essentials of Subtype Analysis; Neuropsychological Assessment of Children: A Treatment-Oriented Approach; Nonverbal Learning Disabilities: The Syndrome and the Model; Neuropsychological Validation of Learning Disability Subtypes;* and *Learning Disabilities and Psychosocial Functioning: A Neuropsychological Perspective.*

Jerel E. Del Dotto, Ph.D., is Division Head, Division of Neuropsychology, Henry Ford Hospital, Adjunct Assistant Professor of Psychology at Wayne State University, and Adjunct Associate Professor of Psychology at the University of Windsor. He is a consulting editor for *The Clinical Neuropsychologist* and the *Journal of Clinical and Experimental Neuropsychology.* He has published as well as presented papers at scientific meetings in the areas of child neuropsychology and learning disabilities.